The

Perfe

MEMO

Write Your Way
to Career Success!

Patricia H. Westheimer

Park Avenue

Perfect Memo
Write Your Way to Career Success!
©1995 Park Avenue Publications

An Imprint of JIST Works, Inc.
720 North Park Avenue
Indianapolis, IN 46202-3431
Phone: **317-264-3720** - Fax **317-264-3709**

Library of Congress Cataloging-in-Publication Data

Westheimer, Patricia H.
    The perfect memo : write your way to career success!
    Patricia H. Westheimer.
        p.   cm.
    Includes index.
    ISBN 1-57112-064-5
    1. Business writing.   2. Memorandums.   I. Title.
    HF5718.W47   1995   94-28472
      658.4'53—dc20   CIP

99 98 97 96 95 94   1 2 3 4 5 6 7 8 9

Printed in the United States of America.

ISBN 1-57112-064-5

BEFORE

Most people dread writing because they:

- ☐ Don't know where to start

- ☐ Feel the need to impress

- ☐ Think the written word is more difficult than the spoken word.

AFTER

SPEAKWRITE™ teaches you how to:

- ☐ Express your message fully

- ☐ Organize your ideas effectively

- ☐ Write your memos confidently.

The Perfect MEMO!

PREFACE

PREFACE

It's 3 p.m., and you're tired. You have to draft a memo by 5 p.m. to all department heads telling them to attend an urgent meeting at noon the next day.

Panic sets in. Memories of junior high school English and red correction marks flood your mind. Suddenly, your previously crisp mind and sharp pencil are on terminal HOLD. You're blocked, trapped, and terrified. Your palms are wet, you look at the clock, and you begin to write. But where do you begin? What do you say? And how?

You start, "Dear...," but then you remember it's a memo, not a letter. Frantically you search your files for memorable memos written by your colleagues, but all you find are minutes of the last board meeting and notes for the next newsletter. It's up to you now. But how?

Then you remember your colleague who works on the third floor. She knows how to write. You dash to her office hoping she'll share some of her secrets. Is she under a magic spell, or does she say some special incantation? How does she know the way to write her winning words, the ones that earned her the promotion last month?

"Sally," you begin, "will you help me write this memo?"

Every day business people face this same dilemma. They have to write, but they don't know how. They put words down, knowing the words aren't the right ones, hoping no one will notice. But people DO notice. Millions of dollars and thousands of hours are lost each week on words that never communicate exactly what needs to be said. Sentences are so lengthy and awkward that readers rarely have time to sift through them for the crucial message.

Now, think about the next memo you have to write. Are you looking forward to composing it? Probably not. Most people dread writing projects because they:

- ☐ Don't know how to begin

- ☐ Struggle to find the right words to use

- ☐ Worry about organization

- ☐ Wrestle with proper punctuation and spelling.

Writing is difficult. However, it doesn't have to take the enormous energy that most people expend only to end up with mediocre results.

There is another way. The SPEAKWRITE™ SYSTEM shows you how to streamline your writing. If you follow my functional formulas, then promotions, increased self-confidence, and newly created challenges will soon become yours.

CONTENTS

CHAPTER 3

CHAPTER 4

CHAPTER 5

CHAPTER 6

The Perfect MEMO!

1

INTRODUCTION: THE SPEAKWRITE SYSTEM

One of the greatest misuses of corporate time and money occurred when a company president decided his top-ranking salesperson needed to learn how to write. He investigated various classes, seminars, and consultants. After careful deliberation, he called the salesperson into his office and *strongly* recommended that she attend a full semester course in traditional English grammar.

What a waste! This already overworked employee had to attend a four-hour weekly class consisting of drills and lengthy lectures in past participles, obscure tenses, and other unnecessary information.

She arrived at my office exhausted and more confused than ever. "I don't see what all of this has to do with my writing. Now I can't even write a phrase without stopping to diagram it. Help!"

Maybe you think you need a grammar class, but wait. You don't. SPEAKWRITE will teach you all you need to know about writing.

What is SPEAKWRITE? It's a five-step recipe for writing.

1. Speak It.

2. Plan It.

3. Format It.

4. Write It.

5. Refine It.

Then you're finished. Once learned, SPEAKWRITE constitutes all action plan for memos and other kinds of writing: letters, reports, lengthy proposals, and projects—almost anything you have to write.

The exciting thing about SPEAKWRITE is how it lets you write the way you always wanted to but believed you couldn't, or were told you shouldn't. Most business writers think they have to use pompous, wordy language to sound important and get their messages taken seriously. Actually, the opposite is true.

Consider the difference between the following memo excerpts:

```
It is realized that you will have to effect numerous
modifications to current procedures expeditiously.
```

or

```
You will have to change current procedures at once.
```

Which memo would you want to receive? Why? The first might work fine for a Ph.D. dissertation on management, but the second gets the point across much more directly and powerfully.

SPEAKWRITE offers a practical plan to banish your writing troubles. Follow this five-part process and you're on your way to being the writer you've always admired. Many very fine business writers admit they don't have fancy techniques. They keep their writing simple. They write the way they speak and stop when they've said enough. A group of successful corporate presidents agreed that the three most important aspects of their writing include brevity, clarity, and personal warmth.

THOSE MEMOS YOU'LL REMEMBER . . . AND WRITE. When was the last time you received a well-written memo? Or wrote one? Can you recognize a well-written memo?

My five-part plan produces the results you want. What's this method? Speak It; Plan It; Format It; Write It; Refine It. How long does it take? Only as long as it takes you to read this book! You will see how to remove all the stuffy words and complex phrases from your writing and shift from pompous to powerful, from meaningless to memorable.

Who can use these tips? Anyone who communicates on paper! That spans everyone from corporate executives to budding entrepreneurs. Speakwriting memos is the one way to keep your message clear, your image up, and your writing time down. When asked, most people claim that writing feels painful, takes too much time, and rarely accomplishes results. That's because most writers start with no real plan and write words suitable for a doctoral thesis, but not for a 60-second memo. They lose their audience before they begin. No wonder writing feels so awkward. Writers never learn a way to make it easy! Our English teachers were supposed to teach us how to write. But they didn't! They taught us how to edit. Now, I'm giving you the opportunity to write. And as you'll soon see, it's very easy!

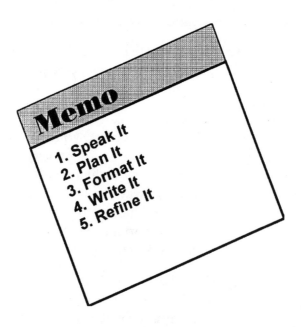

My business-writing career started ten years ago with a short ad I placed in a local paper: "Let me teach you how to write." One person answered: He was a bank manager, and he had to write employee evaluations. He didn't know how to write them, and he couldn't admit it on the job. Not that anyone there could help, he told me during our first, confidence-building meeting. Three hours later he put together the finest employee evaluation he'd ever imagined—AND HE DID IT HIMSELF!

What I showed him was far from complex; he mastered the tools quickly. So can you. You were motivated to pick up this book: that's the biggest step. It reveals your openness to looking at the way you write. Clear communication is essential in the business world. When corporations and organizations call me to teach their employees how to write, some participants are resistant. Others are eager. They want to know how to make the task of writing easier.

The interesting thing about these self-perceptions is that the opposite is usually closer to the truth. The self-styled "good writers" are usually the ones who turn out lengthy memos filled with "businessese" that no one wants to wade through or try to understand. The less confident people who show up for my seminars can usually produce the same message as their more pretentious colleagues, in half the space and with half the syllables, and no one misses their message. Why? Because they rely upon their ears as their guide to effective writing. They haven't been brainwashed, or business-washed, into thinking that they have to sound unusually educated or superior on paper. As a result, they communicate much more clearly, naturally, and correctly.

In a nationwide survey by a communications consulting firm, 79 percent of responding executives listed the ability to write as the single most neglected skill in business, 53 percent rated their own writing ability as poor, and 59 percent rated the correspondence they received as poor or fair. The saddest fact of all was that

60 percent of those queried said they spend nine or more hours a week—one full work day—on business correspondence.

That would be fine, even commendable, if the time spent yielded good results. But customarily it doesn't. Managers, administrators, and secretaries complain that much of their writing time involves agonizing and redoing rather than creating and refining. Even worse, most claim that when they are finished, they are not satisfied with what they have written. To brush up on their writing skills, some people take evening courses in writing, others read books about writers, but few feel any real progress with their seemingly impossible skill.

The rise in the demand for writing specialists has been phenomenal. "Please come back," plead my participants after a four-hour training session in effective writing skills. "We need people like you." Luckily, their employers feel the same way. This growing awareness of the need for better writing on the job has generated a huge demand for writing classes. They do produce results.

The first thing I tell my seminar participants is that writing isn't magical or mystical. Certainly writing the great American novel might be so, but not writing on the job. And they don't have to enroll in extensive technical courses, either. Learn a few principles, and transform your writing today, not tomorrow. My clients do, and you can too.

In this book I'm going to give you the same tools I give my clients. All the examples come from actual employment situations. The names have been changed, but the problems are universal. The tips work for them, and they'll work for you. The system is called SPEAKWRITE. When you write with SPEAKWRITE, everything from the shortest memo to the most complex report shows the signs of an accomplished, confident writer—you!

MEMO!

MEMO-RABILIA
WHEN TO WRITE A MEMO

WHEN:	WHEN NOT:
Informal	Formal
Internal	External
Interoffice	Promotional
Inspired	Personal

The Perfect MEMO!

2

SPEAK IT

So you have to write a memo. It's up to you to communicate clearly, concisely, and correctly. But how?

Initially you need to clarify just what a memo is—and isn't. The worst of all writing experiences occurs when employees spend hours composing, only to find that they have missed the main point, haven't targeted their audience, or haven't written in in the proper form and format. Remember, you're writing a memo—not a letter, meeting minutes, or a report.

One of the biggest mistakes you can make is to assume that you are going to turn out perfect copy without thinking about it. This is a great fallacy and will get you into a lot of trouble with your writing. So, during the early planning stage of writing it is important to determine certain vital elements that are going to go into your memo. Four basic questions you need to ask yourself before you begin to write include:

- ☐ Who's my audience?

- ☐ What's my tone?

- ☐ What's my purpose?

- ☐ What results do I want?

Your **audience** receives your message. In memos your audience is usually more than one person. In letters, it's usually an individual.

Tone is the attitude you take toward your writing. It can be light-hearted or serious, but should always be respectful.

Purpose is the reason for writing. Whether you're writing to inform or inquire, you need to stay on target and not confuse your reason for writing.

Results help determine what you want from this memo. For results you ask, "What do I want?" If you successfully ask for what you want, chances are that you'll get it!

The audience is the most important factor in all of your writing. It is also the one area most people overlook.

FINE FORMATS TO FOLLOW

While there are different memo types and forms, which will be discussed, the basic purpose and scope of a memo is definite. A memo is brief, often sent to more than one person (which distinguishes it from a business letter), and deals with a specific topic in a condensed, standard format. So certain questions about length and style are settled for you before you begin. Some companies even have an established standard memo format for you to follow.

One very successful property development company in Pasadena, California, has a company style book for all of its employees. When the office manager brought me in to consult on writing styles and formats, she handed me the company's book. I looked at her with both amazement and appreciation.

"You don't realize how unusual you are," I said. "Why?" she wondered. "Well, most companies make tremendous (and often erroneous) assumptions about their employees' writing abilities. The employees are given no guidelines to follow, and then management wonders why they turn out memos, reports, and correspondence in differing, awkward, incorrect formats. Usually this format is one that the employees had grown accustomed to using while working for another company."

"Our company's president decided many years ago that he wanted a standard format for all of our letters. So, in our style book, he placed all the different letterheads and sizes we have available and indicated which type was to be used for a memo, letter, report, or proposal."

While thumbing through the style book, I noticed that it also indicated that all letters were to be left justified and right-ragged. This attention to detail is extremely important and shows that considerable thought went into its preparation. The book also reproduced formats and indicated how titles and the personnel of the company were to be identified.

That's an excellent example of a company striving for excellence and uniform quality in writing. The contribution that I made was to provide additional guidelines about specific writing styles. In fact, what I added were many of the items that *The Perfect Memo* teaches.

If the company you work for is as enlightened as the one in the preceding example, be grateful. If not, you may want to meet with your coworkers and propose specific principles for memos. Guidelines make your job easier. In addition, they create a classy look for all corporate communication, internal or external. When you create a unified appearance for your business writing, your readers remember you as representing a company with excellent correspondence. These days, that's about the biggest compliment you can receive!

Many writers focus so heavily on how they're going to write that they overlook a valuable asset: their ears. As your first step, ask yourself, "How would I say this?" Later on, worry about the polish. The best memos almost write themselves.

Imagine your staff sitting around a table. If you must write them a memo about a forthcoming meeting, what would you SAY to them if they were there with you right now? Does it "ring" right? A well-tuned sentence is not the one with complicated vocabulary and poetic lyrics. (Save those passages for your novel or your memoirs.) The best business writing sounds like the best business conversation: brief, clear, direct, relaxed.

Actually, memos are the easiest business correspondence to adapt to SPEAKWRITE. By their very design and purpose, they're short. All you have to do is to imagine a brief conversation and put your ideas in writing.

Good conversationalists know that the best conversations occur when they're in tune with their audience, be it one or one hundred people. But how do they do this? Simple. They focus on their listeners. They ask, "Who's out there? What do they want to hear?"

That's known as "awareness" of the audience and is the first vital step in deciding what you're going to say or write.

ANALYZE YOUR AUDIENCE

What's the best way to bridge the gap between speaking and writing? Audience analysis is a good place to begin. You will never speak or write very well if you don't have any information about the people who are out there in front of you. Improperly prepared, you might inadvertently offend them.

What do you need to know to avoid offending? Start with simple demographic data like age, education, income, occupation, and gender. Next, move right along to your audience's attitudes and their familiarity with the subject of your memo.

"Wait a second," you may be about to blurt, "isn't this a bit much? After all, isn't a memo merely a memo?" NO! The best writers respect and reflect their audiences. Furthermore, they motivate their readers.

But you shouldn't worry. You probably already know the information; just become more conscious of it as you write. Consider the impact the following audience analysis factors are likely to have on your message. It'll only take a few moments of your time, and it will be an excellent investment of your energy.

FACTORS TO ANALYZE

- ☐ Age
- ☐ Gender
- ☐ Education
- ☐ Income
- ☐ Occupation
- ☐ Knowledge
- ☐ Attitudes

AGE. This is business, and would-be memo writers better pay careful attention to those aspects of their audiences. If you use as an illustration an issue of interest primarily to people who came of age in the 1960s, you can probably count on not reaching your older or younger memo recipients. If you employ a colloquial expression that you stole from your sweet 16-year-old daughter, don't be surprised when the adults on your distribution list won't take you seriously.

A manager at a major West Coast hotel generated the following memo material. Some of his more sophisticated employees found it juvenile. (Needless to say, the errors in grammar, punctuation, and spelling didn't help him, either.)

> December is turning out to be a far out month for
> the hotel, both occupancy and rate-wise. One of the
> reasons this month will be so good is because of
> the BUSINESS ROUNTABLE GROUP. Everyone associated
> with this group is listed in the FORTUNE 500, some
> of the most classy companies in the world.
>
> What we have here is a fantastic opportunity. With
> over 400 people paying to use our facilities they
> will also be checking out our property for some of
> their future business meetings. By doing what we do
> best, being friendly, efficient and professionals,
> the business we could generate in the years to come
> is endless.
>
> SO LET'S ALL PITCH IN AND DO THE BANG UP JOB THAT
> WE ARE CAPEABLE OF DOING!!!!!!!!!!!!!!!!!!!!!!!!!!

GENDER. As for gender, knowing to whom you are writing creates a difference in your tone and expression. Writing to the members of an all-female lunch club has a different feel from writing to all the employees who park in Lot 8. Always read your memos as though they were sent to you. Do you feel left out, offended, or included? Is there a question in your mind about what is said?

EDUCATION. Just because you are writing to a well-educated audience, you don't have to use sophisticated, academic language.

When analyzing the readability levels of our newspapers and periodicals, we find that the actual wording is not at the educational level that the readers possess. What does this mean? Knowledgeable editors and writers know that in order for an audience to understand and quickly act on the information, the writing cannot be at the level of a doctoral thesis. It also means that in no way are you showing yourself as undereducated when you use a less than doctoral level to get your point across.

In fact, an interesting experience occurred in a sophisticated employee benefits company. The editor of the company newsletter explained that she took over the job from a woman who was determined to write a newsletter to attorneys in "legalese." This former editor had written with the most long-winded expressions she could find, thinking that this was the manner in which attorneys wished to be addressed. When this new, enlightened editor took over, she wanted to change things around, so she told the staff to write their articles in "plain English."

The staff rebelled. They said that attorneys would never respect the information; they would think it an insult to their intelligence; the newsletter would never again be credible.

The new editor stood her ground. "Let's try it for one issue and see what happens," she told her staff. The results were amazing. When I interviewed her, she said, "I got more thank-you letters and letters of praise for this particular issue than ever in my newsletter-editing career. One attorney wrote, "Thank you for writing to us in a very readable style. It was the most interesting newsletter we have ever received. Keep up the good work."

The preceding example should tell you something about the educational level of your audience. We'll discuss later, in more detail, relaxing stuffy language. It is important, however, to realize from the very beginning, that regardless of the educational level of your audience, you still need to communicate to them in clear, simple, conversational English.

Governmental agencies are notorious for the amount of gobbledygook included in their memos. The next couple of paragraphs are full of it:

> There have been incidents wherein tort claims have
> been filed alleging that personal effects contained
> in seized vehicles have been lost or stolen while
> the vehicles were in our custody. Other problems
> have developed with seized merchandise being left
> in vehicles and the merchandise inadvertently being
> released when the vehicle is claimed by the owner/
> driver.
>
> Effective immediately the procedures contained
> herein will be utilized when a vehicle is seized or
> detained. Section 405 of the local Policies and
> Procedures Manual will be modified to reflect these
> guidelines. I&C Information Bulletin [sic] No. 14
> has been superseded by the instructions contained
> herein.

You don't even have to reorganize; all you have to do is simplify:

> Tort claims have been filed showing that personal
> property in seized vehicles has been lost or stolen
> while we were in charge of the vehicles. Other
> problems have occurred when seized merchandise is
> left inadvertently in the vehicle.
>
> Effective immediately use the following procedures
> when a vehicle is seized or detained. We will
> modify Section 405 of the local policies and
> procedures manual to reflect these guidelines.
> These instructions will supersede the IBC Bulletin
> No. 14.

This revised memo is more concise and easily understood regardless of the reader's education level.

INCOME. How can income affect your audience? Let's say you're in charge of the charity drive in your company this year. The chief executive officer wants employee participation improved by a percentage large enough to win an award. You plan to kick off the campaign with a persuasive memo, but you have a problem. Employees on the lower end of the salary scale have started to complain that they can't possibly increase their contributions. If you are aware of their objections, you can write to them sympathetically and persuasively. Income is an important audience analysis factor.

I remember that when I was on the teaching staff of an independent school in the northeastern United States, the headmaster, around holiday time, sent a memo to all the staff, encouraging us to give substantial contributions to a charity drive. This particular charity was a favorite of his, and he also happened to be chairman of the charity drive for that year. The memo was written in an authoritarian style which assumed that because he was our headmaster, we were also to be loyal to him and his cause. His tone indicated that we would quite willingly give a substantial part of our Christmas bonus to support this "worthy" cause.

Well, he had not stopped to realize that his salary was many times greater than ours. We were underpaid to begin with, and his increased demand on the month's salary that we needed the most came with little sensitivity to our income levels. This memo, again, missed its audience and in turn created hostility toward him and his cause. He wrote:

```
Date:           December 4, 19XX
To:             Everyone
From:           Charlie
Subject:        CHRISTMAS DONATIONS

This Christmas, All Cause Charity, where I am
Chairman, is in need of contributions. Because we
are in the gift giving season, and also because we
are in the last month of the year—a time when
people start thinking about tax deductions—I would
greatly appreciate it if you would give a generous
amount of your Christmas bonus to this worthwhile
cause. Merry Christmas!
```

OCCUPATION. People speak various occupational languages. If, for example, the computer hardware engineers can't comprehend the jargon of the software analysts' suggestions, that means trouble. You may be a manager whose memos must go to different departments. What are you going to do with your writing to get through to everyone? Jargon can't do the job unless everybody understands the same dialect!

If you weren't an airline flight attendant, could you figure out this information update, issued by the attendants' local labor union?

```
The last two updates gave examples of violations
of the 8 in 24 hour rule. Remember this is a
rolling 24 hour period exclusive of deadhead,
limo, duty rig, pushback or tow in. The flight
duty is termed "hard" flying and the only
scheduled or rescheduled flight time is counted,
overflying not included.
```

The same philosophy applies to acronyms. How many times have you received a memo from a different department full of acronyms which are familiar to that department but unknown to you? If you're passing around an *intra*office memo where everyone's familiar with the initials, fine. But this is not correct for *inter*office memos. Avoid memos like this if you have to send them out of your department:

Recently, the APB malfunctioned, causing a chain reaction among the TRQ's, CEBs, and the APs. Please, when using these machines, follow all instructions and make sure that all the machines contain enough SOL, TONE, and RALDO to finish your Job. Have TLC with the machines! Thanks.

KNOWLEDGE. Another audience analysis aspect involves reader knowledge of your subject. When readers are familiar with your topic, you won't need to write in great detail. In these cases, concentrate on succinctness. Try this technique: imagine there's a charge for each word you use, as though you're sending a telegram. Your need for brevity will improve your writing. I've read memos that began, "As you already know," or, "To refresh your memory." Leave these phrases out. They could insult your reader who probably remembers your topic quite clearly. Use your writing to give your readers new information that they need in order to make a decision, take some action, or get on with their work. Any "stale" or background material can be attached to the back of your clear, crisp, concise memo.

But what do you do about an audience that's not knowledgeable? Attempt to assess the exact extent of their familiarity with your material and fill in the empty areas accordingly. That's difficult, though, especially when the knowledge levels within a given group are diverse.

If this applies to your particular predicament, you can choose from a couple of alternatives: either subdivide the group, and devise several specific memos, one for each unit; or compose a single comprehensive message aimed at the large group's least knowledgeable and perhaps less educated members. One office manager wrote this:

```
To:       All Staff
From:     Tina
Date:     April 28, 19XX
Subject:  COMPANY CAR

The company car has been in great demand. Please
turn in your log reports promptly so we can keep
track of where and when the car has been used.

TE: dm
```

She kept her language simple, neither offending nor confusing any of her readers.

ATTITUDES. Audience attitudes have been left until last because all the previous factors affect them. You need to understand your readers' attitudes. How does the audience feel about your topic? Is their attitude positive, neutral, or negative?

Whether the attitude is positive or negative, however, the important point is that ignorance of audience attitude can get you into trouble as a writer. Nothing is more discouraging than receiving a memo that's been written with nobody in mind. It can cause your colleagues to feel neglected, discounted, and downright insulted! Win them over with a personalized, individualized approach, and they'll look forward to reading your memos!
Keep the following "quickie" questions uppermost in your mind. They will keep you focused in on your audience:

☐ Who will read my memo?

☐ What positions do they hold?

☐ How well are they acquainted with the subject matter?

☐ What special interests or personal preferences do they have?

☐ What do I want from them:
Action?
Approval?
Appreciation?

☐ How do they feel about my topic?

☐ How are they likely to react to it?

TACKLING TONE

Choose your words and phrases to fit your audience and the occasion, exactly as you would if you were giving a speech. In that way you let people know you're talking to THEM, not just to ANYONE.

What specifically is tone? It's your style of speaking, the inflections, mood, level of formality or informality you use in communicating. The tone you employ with the president of your company might not work as well with your closest colleague. Tone is just as important in writing as it is in speaking. Remember that your writing is a marketing document. You're selling yourself, your company, your ideas. Keep your tone upbeat, positive, and warm, to present both you and your topic most favorably.

Tone is also the attitude you take toward your topic. Look at the two memos that follow. Pay attention to how the writer (the same person wrote both) has adjusted the tone to fit the audience.

```
To:       Sara Shamblin
From:     Betty Shearer
Date:     March 2, 19XX
Subject:  CORPORATE ADVERTISING
```

We have had occasions to use the corporate advertising group for reprinting of several pieces of promotional literature recently. As you can see from the attached analyses, in each case there has been a substantial penalty to Concepts, Inc. for having materials printed in-house.

In the case of the distributor products catalog, the half we are charged is competitive with commercial rates, but the total cost to Concepts, Inc. including what was picked up in Lee's budget was substantially higher. We have already committed to the corporate advertising group to have several other pieces printed and will, of course, honor those commitments; however, unless you have strong feelings to the contrary, we will plan to do future printing locally. We will get quotes from the corporate group periodically to ensure that the economics have not changed.

cc: Allen Miller

```
To:       Allen Miller
From:     Betty Shearer
Date:     March 30, 19XX
Subject:  SALES  CONFERENCE
```

The Sales Conference will be a useful time to get a feel for our business from the people in the field. I attached an agenda for your information.

I have asked Kathy, my assistant, to check your schedules, as well as Cue's, to see if we can hold our Board of Directors meeting on the 8th before the conference dinner.

Let's discuss details when I return to the office on April 23.

cc: Sara Shamblin

The second memo has a more informal and congenial tone. The writer uses personal pronouns, consciously includes the audience in her text, and breaks up the information into smaller, more easily readable paragraphs.

If you're uncertain about tone, consider your mood. Mood often is the same as tone. The only problem with keeping them parallel is that you might be in an unpleasant mood, yet have to write a memo in a friendly or respectful tone. It's extremely important not to let your mood of the moment negatively influence the tone in your memo.

For instance, a supervisor asks you to write a memo immediately. You don't want to, but she's your supervisor, so you have to. Now, the preferable thing to do is to write that memo in an upbeat manner, rather than in a resentful way. Express your displeasure in another way, not in the memo that carries your signature and reputation. Too many people let their feelings leak out in inappropriate places in their writing. Such a lapse can cloud your communication and cause problems in your career. These negative memos can find a permanent place in the writer's employee file—just where you don't want them.

Another word for tone is attitude. Let's say you have a positive, upbeat attitude that comes across in a readable, likable way in your memos. That's a highly desirable, rare asset. But suppose your attitude on a particular day isn't very positive. You cast pessimism or resentment in your memos. Your readers can see beyond your words. The slightest tinge of negativity can cause an unfavorable reaction. You want that memo to carry a positive attitude; therefore, you have to write as if it were the most important message you've ever written in your life.

```
                NEGATIVE

To:       Everyone
From:     J. P. Fill
Date:     April 24, 19XX
Subject:  WORKING HOURS

There are the hours we want you to work:

    8:00 am - 12:00 noon
    1:00 pm -  5:00 pm

There will be no overtime paid unless your
supervisor approves it.


                POSITIVE

To:       Everyone
From:     John Fill
Date:     April 24, 19XX
Subject:  WORKING HOURS

These are our standard working hours:

8 am - 12 pm
1 pm -  5 pm

If you have to put in extra time, please consult
your supervisor beforehand. Keep up the great work!
```

The tones that work best in business writing are the same ones that work well in relationships: warm, upbeat, positive, friendly, enthusiastic. Since your writing is your ambassador on paper, it's critical that you project a positive, personal image.

Since people do business with those they like and respect, using an appropriate tone is critical to projecting your positive image.

WATCH OUT FOR HUMOR AND SARCASM. There are two tones in memos that I discourage. One is humor, and the other is sarcasm.

Some people have a terrific sense of humor, and you may be one of them. However, humor is very individual, and what's funny to you might be offensive to your reader. Therefore, memos aren't really the place for humor; leave that for your conversation at lunch. Give your memo the respectful, yet personal, tone of someone who's conveying an interesting, important message.

The other tone I recommend avoiding is sarcasm. Sarcasm has a cutting edge and is not at all pleasant to read. No one in your company is naive enough to miss a sarcastic intent in your memo. The following memo was scrawled in black felt pen across the back of a large hotel's personnel action form:

```
TO:        Department Heads
FROM:      Controller

If your employees want their vacation check in
advance then circle the G.D. box! Is that too
hard? I can't make it any simpler for you!
```

The controller could have written:

```
To:       Department Heads
From:     Tom
Date:     February 20, 19XX
Subject:  ADVANCE VACATION CHECKS

Be sure your employees mark the appropriate box to
receive their advance vacation check. Thanks for
your help.
```

Instead of offending or degrading, the writer should attract the reader's attention with a positive, upbeat attitude and tone. That's the kind of memo that people look forward to reading and, most of all, respect.

In my writing seminars, after getting to know the participants for about four hours, I have them submit writing samples for my critique. It usually isn't difficult to identify individual attitudes since people's personalities usually surface within five minutes. It's no accident that even without seeing names at the bottom of these writing samples, I can tell who produced the positive sample, who the negative, who the sarcastic, and who the inappropriately off-color one.

If you're feeling down, try writing to lift your spirits. Draft your memo as though you were in the best possible frame of mind. Writing can turn your mood around! Unfortunately, most people feel that writing turns their mood down. Actually, it can uplift and energize you. It may even make you the most popular person in your firm. There's no doubt that it's that kind of attitude that attracts people to you, your writing, and your work.

WRITING TO SUPERIORS AND SUBORDINATES.

In a routine memo your tone probably won't cause many problems. The rules are fairly straightforward. If you're not the top executive in your company, you'll probably recommend, request, or suggest. It's usually only the ultimate superiors who direct. All others take a softer tone. The superintendent of one of the ten largest school districts in the United States wrote the following memo. Although he doesn't belabor his authority, what he wants is implicit. It's clear he's number one!

```
Subject:   STAFF DEVELOPMENT AND TRAINING
           ADVISORY COMMITTEE

The district is establishing certificated and
classified staff development and training advisory
committees. All employees will have representation
on these committees. You have been nominated to
serve on the Certificated Staff Development and
Training Advisory Committee.

As a district, we are committed to establishing an
effective staff development and training program for
all district employees. These advisory committees
are an integral part of this program. I hope that
you will consent to participate as a member of this
very important committee.
```

Ten years ago you'd never see personal pronouns in business writing. Today they're well accepted and establish a much more natural tone than the awkward "one" or "the undersigned." However, you can go too far with your references. The following memo was written by a bank employee who got much too personal:

```
M, great to see you last night. I love your new
hair style. Since everyone is in agreement I see no
reason to continue printing these two forms. Should
the ORC agree with this, BS and SB will need to be
notified to obsolete their respective forms. Let's
get together for drinks and discuss.
```

What's wrong with this memo? It suffers from:

❏ Inappropriate personal comments

❏ Too many initials

❏ Mixed tone

❏ Inappropriate close.

If someone else needed the information or the contacts, they'd never know whom to ask. Memos are for "insiders," but inappropriate camaraderie can undermine your overall purpose, authority, and professionalism.

Tone causes the biggest problem when the subject is delicate. The more sensitive the reader or the issue, the more you will have to promote goodwill. Tactlessness in writing is destructive. When emotions are involved, a single misused word can make an enemy, as can an inappropriate or misguided tone. That's all the more reason to examine your attitude carefully before you write. Make sure it's either neutral or positive—but most of all, respectful.

Imagine that you're the head of a governmental agency. What would you think of an organization that sent out this memo?

```
At our last meeting, you requested agenda topics
for a meeting of the Committee on Atmosphere and
Oceans. I certainly support this inter-agency
grouping as it may serve as an appropriate forum
for directing our marine technology needs and
concerns.
```

This memo has little to recommend it. The first sentence is lazy; it merely repeats the request. The real trouble comes with the second sentence which attempts goodwill but backfires: "certainly" is a needless intensifier; "inter-agency grouping" is pompous phrasing; "needs and concerns" doubles a word to form a redundant phrase. Finally, "I certainly support this" is undermined by the phrase "it may serve." "May serve"? The issue isn't whether the group should exist. What should it discuss? In this revision the second sentence is dropped, making the first one do more of the work:

```
As you requested, I am submitting some agenda
topics for the meeting of the Committee on
Atmosphere and Oceans.
```

Isn't that more direct? The tone is both warmer and better focused. More important, the readers are likely to respond positively.

Another way of establishing attitude in your writing is through the conscious selection of pronouns such as "you, your, we, us." Try to use these in place of "I," "me," your name, your own company. Instead of writing, "I have decided that my company will be closed over Labor Day weekend," why not say, "We will close over Labor Day weekend. Enjoy your holiday!"

PRACTICE READER-BASED WRITING. The latest trend today suggests using reader-based writing, meaning that you write for your reader rather than for yourself. This is a critical orientation to remember at the beginning of any writing project.

One of the most common things I see in memos submitted to me is that most of them begin with and are flooded with the pronoun "I." Now, how important is "I" to the reader? Not very. Successful salespeople know how to target their product or their service to their customer. This is the key to get them to buy and use the product. It's the same with effective writers. So, instead of using "I," "me," "us," or "we," why not focus instead on "you," "your," client's name, or client's concern? Look at the following memo and notice how preoccupied the writer is with the word "I." Then, change it to a "you" orientation and see the shift.

Here's a quick tip. If it's too difficult to write directed toward your audience, direct your first draft toward yourself. Then when you revise your memo, change your orientation from writer-centered to reader-centered.

```
MEMO—NO-NO!

To:       Office Manager
From:     Ms. Donaldson
Date:     April 24,19XX
Subject:  DEDUCTIONS


I was reviewing your department's travel deductions
and I found too many unverified deductions. Please
consult me concerning these errors.


          MEMO—YES-YES!

To:       Office Manager
From:     Rita
Date:     April 24, 19XX
Subject:  REIMBURSEMENTS


When you travel on business keep a log of your
business expenses. We can reimburse you faster if
there are fewer unverified vouchers. Thanks for
your help!
```

SPEAKING AND WRITING: THERE IS NO DIFFER-ENCE. There's a myth that writing and speaking are totally separate functions, that the best conversations have nothing to do with the best letters, or memos. There's no logical reason for such a myth. That's what's wrong with writing. Writing has drifted so far from natural, casual conversational speaking that no one can understand what most writers mean. They sound so stuffy and pompous that you'd never tolerate them in a conversation. Yet you have to put up with them on paper.

Another reason we don't trust our natural writing voice is that many schools fail to build confidence in writing skills. Red marks fill papers; degrading grades destroy enthusiasm and confidence before the student can build up confidence or love of writing. So we resort to clichés, "businessese," fancy jargon, and others' styles because we've never learned to build or trust our own style. Remember that a memo is:

❐ Concise

❐ Compact

❐ Casual.

If you honor these three guidelines, then your memo writing will be painless and powerful.

Look at these two memos, both written by successful businesses. See for yourself which tone works better for the subject matter and intended receiver:

```
To:       Peter Fisher
From:     Mary Butler
Date:     April 24, 19XX
Subject:  NEW MARKET RELEASES

In reference to our agreement on November 17, 1994
regarding New Market Releases, it has come to my
attention that new market has been released to Mike
Townsend without being issued to the Homes Passed
Clerk first. Attached is a copy of Mike Townsend's
DAR listing the new market address. To ensure timely
processing, it is imperative that the Homes Passed
Clerk receive the New Market Releases before other
departments. Thank you.


To:       All Area Distribution
From:     Maggie Well
Date:     March 5, 19XX
Subject:  ACTIVITIES

On Wednesday, March 20, we will have a Benefit Booth
on company-sponsored activities. Please encourage
your employees to stop and pick up information on
upcoming events.

The Committee is also recruiting new members to
join, and we hope your department will be
represented.

If no one from your department volunteers or
expresses an interest, try to encourage
participation.

Please let me know your thoughts on this.
```

Imagine that it's 4 p.m. You've just received both of these memos. Which one is easier to read? Why? If you do nothing more than read the first line of each memo, you will see how stuffy, awkward, and routine the phrase "In reference to . . ." sounds as opposed to "On Wednesday, March 20, we will have a Benefit Booth on company-sponsored activities."

One memo sounds stuffy, and the other natural. One is awkward, the other conversational. In either case it's fortunate that they're both short. But the second has an additional advantage. Just look at it for a minute and notice the layout. Why does it catch your eye and seem more pleasing than the first? The reason relates to the concept of "white space." White space results when the writer breaks up the different topics into neatly written and briefly stated paragraphs. It allows the reader to absorb the material more easily by presenting smaller "bite-sized" chunks.

In school, you were taught not to have one-sentence paragraphs. This concept is not practical in today's business world. The way in which your eye perceives a writing "structure" is just as important as the way a paragraph reads. You were also taught to develop each paragraph as a topic sentence with examples to support and collaborate. A memo, because it is brief, does not need numerous supporting facts and circumstances. A memo should consist of facts that your reader can absorb quickly and easily. The reader can then respond, make a decision, and get on with the rest of a busy schedule.

This is all a memo is intended to accomplish, and that's what the second memo does so well.

WHAT'S YOUR PURPOSE?

It's important to have your purpose in mind before you begin to write. Are you writing to inform, respond, refute, inquire, direct, or persuade? Once your purpose is clear, the organization and focus of your memo become easier to determine.

One of the main pitfalls in memo writing is to try to make your memo do too much at one time. A memo that attempts to give information on a new topic, respond to a previous problem raised at a staff meeting, and raise issues to consider for the next meeting confuses the reader and weakens each topic.

The following memo illustrates this problem:

```
To:       Everyone
From:     Mr. Canley
Date:     May 3, 19XX
Subject:  OVERTIME, LUNCHES, NEXT WEEK'S MEETING,
          BUDGETS, PROFIT-SHARING

We have been very busy lately, and I haven't been
able to get out several memos, so I decided to
condense some major problems into one memo.

Overtime—It's great that so many of you are putting
in extra hours, keep up the good work.

Lunches—Many of you are taking long lunches and
making up for the time after 5 pm. I'm glad you are
conscientious about making up the time, but I'd
prefer that you didn't take the extra time at lunch.
It's a burden to have to try and find you after
lunch when some of you don't even show up until 2!

Next meeting—At next Monday's meeting we will
discuss flow charts, cold calling, new benefits, and
our quarterly finances—please be prepared on all of
the topics—more to follow on this.

Budgets—many departments' budgets are way over their
maximum. We are trying to cut back everywhere.
Please be considerate of your supervisor when she
asks you to conserve on paper, travel expenses, etc.

Profit-sharing—The profit-sharing allocations are
out. See Mary for your copy.
```

To solve this problem, write a separate memo on each topic listed in the subject line. Make each of your memos have a single focus and a single purpose. Imagine that you are the recipient, not the writer! Make your subject lines be as interesting, eyecatching, and appealing as possible. A bland subject line such as "LUNCHES" could be appealingly replaced by "LONGER LUNCHES."

RESULTS: HOW TO GET WHAT YOU WANT

Finally, consider "results." That is, before you write, always ask yourself, "What do I want?" Do you want an appointment, a raise, a contract, a telephone call?

If you can't come up with a need for writing, maybe you don't have to write at all! But most of us do want something, and it's critical to keep that fact in mind before you begin to write.

Determine your:

❐ Audience

❐ Tone

❐ Purpose

❐ Results.

Ask yourself these key questions: who is my audience, what is my tone, why am I writing, and what do I want? Answering these four questions helps you focus before you begin to write.

The Perfect MEMO!

3

PLAN IT

"Okay," you're thinking, "now I'm ready to write." You're probably also saying to yourself, "I've done all the preliminary work, researched my audience, determined my purpose, written out what I want, now isn't it the time to sketch a quick outline, write my memo, and stop?" The answer is NO. Why not? Because the latest research shows that the most important stage of all in your writing is what writing researchers call "The Prewriting Stage."

Prewriting involves techniques for coming up with your ideas and sorting them out, very different from the traditional outlining techniques you were taught in school. Outlining is a left-brain function. It attempts to organize ideas before you even come up with them. Mindmapping, sometimes called clustering, is just the opposite. It hooks into your right-brain which lets you creatively come up with ideas in a random, free-flowing fashion. This process gives you a greater range of ideas and creativity than the traditional outlining structure ever permitted.

In this chapter we'll discuss prewriting techniques which include:

☐ Brainstorming

☐ Mindmapping

☐ Freewriting

☐ Organizing.

Briefly, brainstorming lets you free-associate your ideas in a random, unstructured form. Mindmapping, sometimes called clustering, allows you to group your topics in a creative, flowing diagram. Freewriting takes these ideas and lets you write them all out without stopping, censoring, editing, or starting over. Soon, you'll see examples of all three.

Organizing lets you take the free-flowing ideas you've created by brainstorming, mindmapping, and freewriting, and put them in a meaningful, powerful order so you can begin to write with direction.

All of these techniques are superior to traditional outlining which assumes you know the order of ideas before you even have them. How absurd!

WHY CAN'T I START?

The reasons why we won't let ourselves start writing is that we think we have to turn out perfect copy the first time. Many people write with someone looking over their shoulder—usually their eighth-grade English teacher!

Some of the reasons why we can't start include:

❏ Writer's block

❏ Writing myths

❏ Stifled creativity

❏ Confidence crunch.

SPEAKWRITE shows you how to break through all of these limitations with brainstorming, mindmapping, freewriting, and organizing to create your perfect memo!

HERE'S HOW TO START

Brainstorming is one of the best methods for getting your ideas on paper initially—before you organize, reorganize, or write. Brainstorming has a releasing, free-flowing feeling. It's a powerful way to loosen up your tightness about writing so that you can begin to create.

Most people compose with two voices simultaneously competing inside them. One's the writer: creative and uncensored; the other's the editor: critical, judgmental, repressive. The problem is that the editor comes into play too early in most people's writing process. This "bad guy" kills off too many good ideas before they ever get on paper. That's not to say that the editorial voice isn't necessary; it's a vital voice, just not in your initial writing stage.

During the first stages of writing, when you're deciding on ideas to insert, be lenient with yourself. Now's the relaxed time when no one's looking—not your boss, your colleagues, not even your junior high school English teacher! You'll discover during these first planning stages that you're much more creative than you ever have given yourself credit for.

The director of a large hospital had to write a memo to his staff about a promotion he'd just received. He was excited about the change but had buried his enthusiasm in a bland, routinely written memo. Luckily, he happened to be in a writing class and brought the about-to-be-sent memo with him. "I know it isn't very interesting," he admitted, "but it's the best I can do. I struggled with it for hours." His memo read like this:

> This is to inform you that effective October 1, 19XX, I have accepted the position of Corporate Vice President, Business Industry Division of Health Services, Inc. In this capacity, my duties will include developing a new division which will be responsible for the marketing and sales of all existing services within the corporation and both hospitals, and the creation of industrial programs.

When he learned that brainstorming is the key to creative memos, his eyes brightened. I saw him begin to write down all his ideas on the topic energetically, nonstop. This is exactly what brainstorming is all about. Fifteen minutes later he dashed off twenty thoughts. He recognized that once he unlocked his creativity, he could transform even the most mundane topic into an eyecatching, fascinating piece of writing. Eventually he revised his memo. First he brainstormed it:

☐ promotion

☐ new opportunities selling new products

☐ giving new opportunities new markets—giving out free samples

☐ expanding old ideas—quotas, rewards, hospital relations

☐ sales incentives, new industries, new people, cutting edge of technology, vacations for good sales, higher wages

Then he rewrote it:

```
I will be accepting the position as corporate Vice
President, Business and Industry Division, Health
Services, Inc. on October 1, 19XX. With my new
position I will be able to create new opportunities,
provide greater sales incentives and establish
different markets. In addition, I will be
responsible for developing a new division. This
division will consist of marketing and sales within
the corporation and both hospitals, plus I will
create new industrial programs.
```

"I always thought I had to delegate all my writing to someone else. Deep down I was sure about the strength of my ideas—I just didn't know how to get them out!" He added, "Now I feel like a 'reborn writer'!"

STORMING YOUR BRAIN

You can brainstorm as effectively as he did. Here are the steps to help you to brainstorm the simplest memo or the most complex piece of writing.

Start by jotting down one insight after another about your topic.

While you're doing this, imagine that you're a reporter holding fast to your five sacred *W*'s and one *H*:

- ❏ WHO (will receive it, will be affected)?

- ❏ WHAT (is it about)?

- ❏ WHY (is it needed)?

- ❏ WHERE (will it occur)?

- ❏ WHEN (are its deadlines scheduled)?

- ❏ HOW (will it be carried out)?

Then get going! Generate as many ideas on your topic as you can. The important point here is that you do no editing at all. An inner voice might shout, "No!" or "That's ridiculous!" or "You already said that!" Ignore it. This is your time to be completely creative and uncensored. You'll have plenty of opportunities to edit and polish. This is like summer vacation—no school rules; have fun!

The manager of a telecommunications firm had to write a memo about sick leave benefits. He was stuck. He tried to turn out a polished product before he had even begun! He was frustrated, so he decided to brainstorm. Suddenly he was excited. He conjured up many more interesting aspects of the issue than he had ever imagined, all because he took the time to brainstorm.

He forgot about the finished product. All he wanted was to put his concepts on paper. Afterwards he admitted his amazement at how many thoughts he had on the subject. Previously, he had felt cut off, trying to get the memo completed quickly. But when he released his mind to flow freely in the right-brain mode, he found that his personal resources were richer than he had ever expected. People who write like this are relieved to discover how much they have to say. No longer does the composition process block or limit them. They learn to trust themselves as a primary source.

BRAINSTORMING

SPEAKING AND WRITING

MAPPING YOUR MIND

A close cousin to brainstorming is a technique called mindmapping. To relax the usual rigidity of writing, I suggest mindmapping. This is a visual representation of the way your mind sorts information. You start with your central idea in the center of your page, then branch your ideas off this core idea. Sometimes mindmapping is called "clustering" because the mind clusters, or lumps, related ideas. The mind doesn't sort information in big and little A's or in Roman Numerals I and II as does an outline. Outlining blocks creativity rather than encouraging it. Mindmapping does just the opposite. It follows your mental process and encourages creativity.

There is no one correct way to mindmap, but here are some general guidelines to help you start.

☐ In the center of your paper, draw a square or a circle.

☐ Inside the circle, write the name of your project, subject of your correspondence, or item you intend to discuss.

☐ Draw branches from the circle, like branches from a tree, to designate your main topics or concerns.

☐ To help identify these topics, you might use the $5W$'s and $1H$. Ask yourself who, what, when, where, why, and how.

☐ Branch off into smaller but related topics.

☐ Don't worry about the organization of your branches; that comes later.

☐ Use different colored pens or pencils to designate related topics.

A group of police officers learning report writing were attentive but still unexcited about writing. Then they heard about mindmapping! They picked up their pens and began to apply the technique to their report writing forms. One officer produced this gem right on the spot:

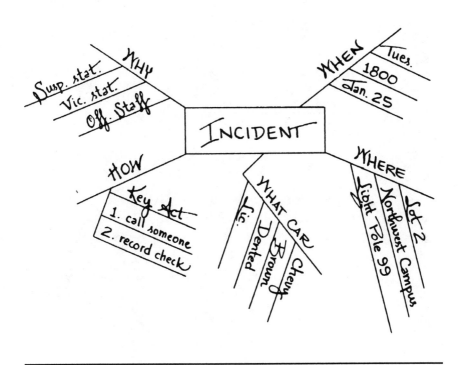

He and his colleagues were excited about this technique. They said it would help them organize and energize their report writing. It can do the same for you! To show you another example, imagine you want to summarize *The Perfect Memo.* One way you could mindmap it appears below.

THE PERFECT MEMO MIND MAP

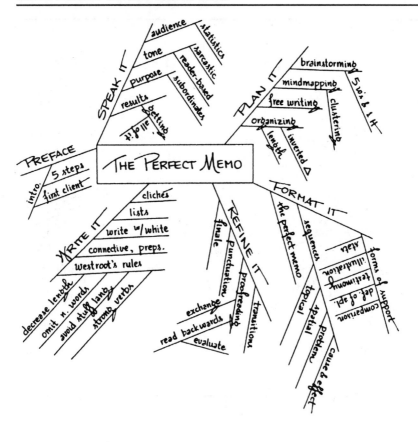

After you've brainstormed or mindmapped, you may have a few final flashes of insight for your memo.

Remember, your brainstorm and mindmap generate the basic building blocks of your memo. They provide the skeleton, the bones, the framework of your subject. Once you're finished with them, much of your work is completed.

What if you run out of ideas? If that happens, and it often does, simply write something down, anything, even if it's unrelated to your subject. Your brain will enjoy this kind of freedom. Once you get in the groove again, your brainstorms, mindmaps, and freewrites will take off. Suddenly, you'll look down at your ideas, and they will have multiplied.

I remember an engineer I worked with on his reports. He said that the things he wrote were so routine and unimaginative the thought of writing bored him unbearably. But once he started brainstorming, he got new angles that enabled him to look forward to this previously dreaded task. At the end of my seminar, he said, "Hey, brainstorming is the best tool I've ever been taught for writing. I don't worry about being blocked anymore. Now I know where and how to get going again. Thanks a lot." I think you'll like this technique, too. It's even simpler than it seems.

FREEING YOUR WRITING

A third prewriting technique to loosen you up and start you off is freewriting. The key to freewriting is writing without an editor or a voice talking to you that wants you to edit, change, and rewrite as you compose. To freewrite, pick up your pen or start your word processor and begin composing without making any changes, adding corrections, or starting over. Ignore punctuation, spelling, grammar, and organization. Let your thoughts flow freely. You'll have time later to go back and revise them. In freewriting, your mind may wander to next month's golf tournament or tonight's dinner. Don't worry about it, just write. Here's an example of freewriting a client composed.

```
FREEWRITING:

gotta to talk about sales projections and etc. I
need memos from you, Sandy, and Jim about sales
projections for the following quarter. Also I want
to think about profit-sharing (Does that include a
trip to Mexico?). We've got to inform employees
about benefits. dental. medical. vacations. Need a
meeting next week.

REVISED:

Joe, let's call a meeting of all managers next
Tuesday and discuss sales projections for the
following quarter. Before the meeting we'll need
input from you, Sandy, and Jim on your own
projections. We also need to think about our profit
sharing fund and to let the employees know about
their benefits. How about getting together Monday to
discuss all of the above?
```

Sometimes it's easier to freewrite after you've brainstormed or mindmapped. You have your ideas; then use each topic to produce sentences, then paragraphs, then your memo! Don't worry about your form, formats, or overall look. Just keep writing as quickly and freely as you can.

Most people say it's easier to edit than to write. So, once you have your rough draft, you can then go back and clean it up. But the hard part's over; you have your copy.

FREEWRITING

☐ WRITE WITHOUT STOPPING
☐ CREATE WITHOUT EDITING
☐ FORMAT DOUBLE-SPACED
☐ ALLOW NO CRITICIZING
☐ LET IT SIT!

ORGANIZING YOUR IDEAS

Okay, now you're finished with brainstorms, mindmaps, and freewrites. What do you do next? You've gotten all your ideas down on paper. Then, suddenly you wake up your editor: "Hey, I need your help now."

You look over your list of all those concepts that poured out of your brain, and you say, "Have I included everything?" Review your list:

❐ What is my memo about?

❐ Why did I write it?

❐ When should I write it?

❐ How will it be answered?

❐ How will it be received?

❐ Who's going to get it?

❐ Who's my audience?

❐ What's my tone?

❐ What's my purpose?

❐ What will be the results?

Now you can celebrate. You've produced the ideas you need for your topic. But you may say, "What will I do with all of these? I have twenty brainstorms and two mindmaps, but all I need to produce is a one-page memo."

Great, now you're going to begin to determine which ideas stay and which ones go. I don't suggest a big black pen or a giant pair of scissors. I do, however, recommend a system of ordering. Number your thoughts in order of importance—to whom? To your reader, of course!

You've done the groundwork—now you need to organize your brainstorms, mindmaps, and freewrites. But how? Most writers organize as they write. Ideas pop into their heads, and they write them down in the order in which they come to them, which sometimes, sadly, is in no order at all. Or it's an order that might make sense at the moment to the harried writer, but might not make any sense to the reader who's in an entirely different mood and mindset from the writer.

Disorganized memos are hazardous. The real problem with poor organization is that it creates unnecessary length—just what you don't want. Think about the best memo you've ever received. Was it

☐ Long or short?

☐ Rambling or direct?

☐ Scrambled or organized?

☐ Muddy or clear?

You probably answered those questions without even thinking. There's no mystery to writing. Just make your memos short, direct, organized, and clear. And stop! Curiously, the mark of punctuation (which we'll cover in more detail later) that most people too seldom use is the period. They want to ramble when they need to STOP! Put in the period!

Now, back to organization. Here you'll learn different styles for organizing and supporting your ideas.

MEMO!

BRAINSTORM

☐ MEMO FOR A COMPUTER PURCHASE

  ☐ existing need
  ☐ old equipment outdated
  ☐ new requirements
  ☐ additional responsibilities
  ☐ cost effective
  ☐ saves time
  ☐ additional functions
  ☐ by end of year

THE INVERTED PYRAMID—YOUR MEMO'S HIDDEN POWER

One way to organize your thoughts is to think of the structure of your memo as an inverted pyramid.

The foundation of this inverted pyramid is the principle of *inductive reasoning.* Simply stated, your conclusion comes first. Next come the how you arrived at your conclusion and the why you support it. The opposite is *deductive reasoning,* which leaves the most important for last, building toward some kind of climax. While this technique might work well in a movie or a novel, it won't do well in a memo. It muddies the communication, and it wastes the time of your busy colleagues and clients. To form your inverted pyramid:

☐ Put your most important point up front.

☐ Focus your audience's attention on it.

☐ Explain it more extensively.

☐ Support and develop it more strongly.

Whatever you do to emphasize your most important point, the top of your memo will contain more substance than the bottom. Thus, it will look and feel like an inverted pyramid.

If you paid five dollars to see a movie, you'd be furious if you knew the ending within the first five minutes. But if you had only five minutes to read an important memo, you'd be amazed if you couldn't find the facts right away. Fiction stories build up suspense; they make you wait. Good business writing does just the opposite; it opens with the most important information and tapers off to the least important. The "bottom" line becomes the top line.

A bank executive flew in from Santa Barbara to consult about her writing. She was concerned about an important memo to her colleague about the print size on the colleague's training slides. After reading two pages of background information, justification, and reasoning, I began to wonder, "When is she going to get to the point?"

Finally, buried on page three, she had written, "I think the typeface should be larger on the slides to make them easier to read." Why didn't she put this in the beginning? She explained that she thought she had to build up her request and lead her reader slowly to the main point.

When I asked her if that's what she wants when she receives memos, she responded, "No! I want them to get to the point right away and not waste my time!" Without any further explanation, she smiled and started her memo with her request. Be bold!

A hotel supervisor once asked, "But what if I'm asking for something that I know my reader doesn't want to give me—like a special parking spot, a day off, or the use of a company car for a day?" In these cases, you might not want to start the memo off immediately with the request. Instead, begin with a single logical reason to prepare the reader.

For example:

> Because I work the late shift, I don't arrive until 4 p.m. By this time, all the company parking spaces are still full from the previous shift. Would you designate some spaces where parking is limited from 9-4, leaving them open for second shift employees?

As often as you can, organize your memos as journalists do, with the most important information up front. That's the critical difference between writing for information (inverted pyramid) and writing for entertainment (pyramid). After you've completed your draft, find the most important information, circle it, and put it as close to the beginning of your memo as you can.

ORGANIZATION

AVOID

Least Important

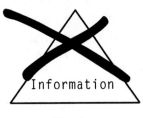

Information

Most

PYRAMID

Mystery story!

USE

Most Important

Information

Important

INVERTED PYRAMID

Not a mystery story!

Then:
Number your ideas—in order of importance.

When you write, think about the one sentence you would keep if you could save only one. Put that sentence right up front—if it's not to be your first sentence (and often it can be), then certainly it belongs in your first paragraph. Remember the following memo tips, and you'll keep strong at organizing your ideas. Always put:

- ☐ Requests *before* justifications

- ☐ Answers *before* explanations

- ☐ Conclusions *before* discussions

- ☐ Summaries *before* details

- ☐ Generalities *before* specifics.

YOU'RE NOT WRITING A MYSTERY STORY!

POINTING OUT PRIORITIES

Look at the following mindmap:

MINDMAPPING

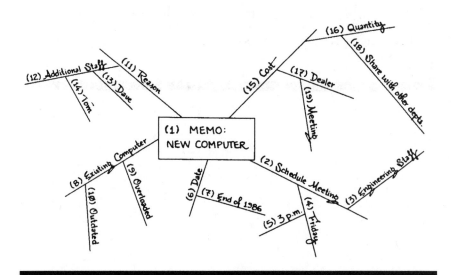

Notice the numbers next to each topic. I've prioritized the topics in the order I felt best for the reader. By numbering your brainstorms or the branches of your maps, you can decide which topics are the most important. You can use these subjects as headers, which we will discuss later, when you actually begin to write your memo. Then when you write, go directly to your primary point. The best organization for brief memos contains these characteristics:

☐ One to three main points, arranged with the most important point first

☐ Several examples to support each point

☐ One or two comments on each example.

Here's an example:

We need to make three major budget cuts. The first will be cutting back on foreign investments. The dollar is not strong now. It can do better domestically.

Second, we will decrease foreign services because of our slowdown in investments. This will free up money to invest elsewhere.

Finally, we will cut back on foreign travel. Since our foreign investments will diminish, we shouldn't have to travel as extensively.

WHAT IF YOU DICTATE?

But what if you dictate? Dictation is a great help to some writers. Dictation speeds up their writing process, breaks writer's block, and allows them to get started when "paralyzed" on how to write a particular paper. While dictation can lend support to your writing, it can also sabotage both you and your secretary's sanity.

Some people buy fancy dictation equipment and begin speaking into it as if they were creating the Great American Stream-of-Consciousness novel. So, rather than receiving a well-organized, carefully formatted sequence of ideas, the secretary gets a tangle of thoughts that contain neither coherence nor logical process of thought.

How can you avoid this problem? Simply by using the same planning stages that all good writers use. Analyze your audience and determine your purpose. All the same strategies and "prewriting" exercises that you undertake as a writer can also be done when you dictate. This allows you to dictate with a plan. Follow your points in order to move logically from one thought to the next.

Secretaries working from dictation equipment say that when the person dictating follows some type of key-word plan, the transcription job becomes much easier. It makes the secretary's job easier, and the final product emerges as much more powerful.

One secretary of a large construction company took me to lunch the other day and related to me her pet peeves about taking dictation. "I would like, just once, to have each dictator listen to the jumble of incoherency I receive in a typical day."

Here is her list of dictating hints she would like each dictator to remember:

- ☐ Make a game plan for the dictation. Most dictators jump from topic to topic with little noticeable relationship between each. A plan also makes rewrites much easier.

- ☐ Use the pause (or stop) button when composing your thoughts. One dictator left the record button on for a full fifteen minutes between paragraphs while he thought of what to say.

- ☐ Turn the record button off when not dictating. When one dictator rode around town, he left the record button on. While he drove, he talked to himself, swore, and worst of all, blared the radio in the background. This made the secretary's job all the more difficult.

- ☐ Be sure to spell out people's names, addresses, and all unfamiliar proper nouns. Nothing infuriates a customer more than to receive a memo with his or her name, address, or other facts misspelled.

One broker reported that a major client called to respond to a proposal he had just received. After commenting that the proposal was well-written and interesting, the client added a "P.S." "Hey Jim, next time I'd like my name spelled properly." The broker looked embarrassed and blushed as he told the story, and admitted that he luckily had a very congenial client.

Valuable contracts have been lost merely because the client's name was misspelled. It is generally perceived as a sign of sloppiness which the client thinks may carry over to the execution of the contract.

The personnel manager of a fast-food chain reported that she had placed an advertisement in a local newspaper for a job that was open in her company. She was swamped with resumes and cover letters. One prospective employee was well qualified for the job but misspelled this personnel manager's name. Angered and upset, she reported that she didn't even call the prospect in for an interview. The reason she gave for this harsh judgment was that "if she was going to misspell my name, what other details would she miss?" I understood her reasoning. Spell everything correctly!

Those are just a couple of pointers about dictation. Whether you handwrite your first copy, dictate it, or type it out on a word processor, all modes work if you feel comfortable using your particular style. Whichever method you use, the underlying principles remain constant. And having a plan to work from is the most important reminder of all.

Artists plan their paintings, potters sketch their products. You, too, as a creative, productive writer now realize the importance of careful planning techniques. They aren't anything that your reader or supervisor will ever see, so have fun and be creative with them. Let your mind drift into areas of inspiration you never knew you had—free yourself up and let yourself enjoy this most important and neglected phase of writing.

The Perfect
MEMO!

4

FORMAT IT

Style confuses many, but format confuses even more people. This section deals with the most up-to-date, simplified information on formatting your memos. Although it may be true that your company has its own format (and if that's the case, by all means use it), many companies don't have a format. Because of this, writers stumble over formats. The memo which follows includes numbers in parentheses to allow you the formatting reasons for each line.

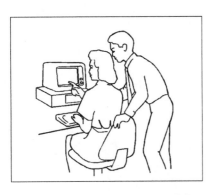

FoRMAT

(1) MEMO

(2) To: (3) All Employees and Volunteers
(4) From: (5) Joan Rightwood
(6) Date: May 16, 19XX
(7) Subject: (8) DEPARTMENTAL SHIFTS

Administrative changes will occur by June 10. These changes will include:

(9) ❏ Human Resources will move to our Communications Building.

(10) ❏ Purchasing will be a separate department.

❏ Word processing will combine with Publications.

Bring your suggestions to our staff meeting on Monday, June 8 at 3:30 p.m.

(11) (no signature)

(12) JR:cc
(13) cc: Jacki Carde
          John Allen
          Eileen Weller

(1) To distinguish this correspondence from any other, type "Memo" at the top of the page. "Memo" is a more contemporary and relaxed word for the more formal word "Memorandom." "Memo" also reflects the informality of the correspondence.

(2) Use "To" as the first of your identification lines. This line comes first because your audience is the most important factor in your writing.

(3) This line refers to the main people who will receive and take action on your memo. Additional interested people are listed below in (13).

(4) Use "From" as the second of your identification lines to identify yourself as the writer.

(5) Here, make sure you identify yourself by name. A department can't write a memo, but a department head can. Plus, you should be proud to have your name on this memo!

(6) The date is important so that the reader understands the urgency of the memo, and when you wrote it. It is also used for filing purposes so include the month, day, and year.

(7) Notice I've used the word "Subject," not "Re" or "Reference." "Subject" is more contemporary; besides, we don't use "Re" in speech.

(8) Make your subject as specific, concise, and appealing as you can. After all, you want to attract your reader to your subject. Capitalize each letter to attract attention. Secretaries also use the subject line for filing purposes. Make these words as appealing and attention-grabbing as you can. Bland subject heads lose readers; lively ones attract them.

(9) The dominant trend in today's paragraph formatting tends toward the block style, with the copy typed flush left and ragged right. Avoid the temptation, if you're using a word processor, of also justifying the right margin. Recent studies have shown that it takes longer to read and comprehend a memo (or letter) if both left and right margins are justified. Also, before word processors became so popular, it was considered technologically advanced to right-justify margins to show everyone that "I have a computer and know how to use it." Today, computers are so commonplace that such is not true. Polished writers now leave a ragged right margin not only to enhance readability, but to show a personalized touch (as if it were hand-typed).

Here's what a right-justified memo looks like:

```
                            MEMO

To:       All Employees and Volunteers
From:     Joan Rightwood
Date:     May 15,19XX
Subject:  ADMINISTRATIVE CHANGES

Administrative changes will occur by June 10. These
changes will include:

    ❑ Human Resources will move to our Communications
      building.

    ❑ Purchasing will be a separate department.

    ❑ Word Processing will combine with Publications.

Bring your suggestions to our staff meeting on Monday,
June 8, at 3:30 p.m.
```

Now look at the same memo right-ragged:

```
                          MEMO

To:        All Employees and Volunteers
From:      Joan Rightwood
Date:      May 15,19XX
Subject:   ADMINISTRATIVE CHANGES

Administrative changes will occur by June 10. These
changes will include:

   ❒ Human Resources will move to our Communications
     building.

   ❒ Purchasing will be a separate department.

   ❒ Word Processing will combine with Publications.

Bring your suggestions to our staff meeting on
Monday, June 8, at 3:30 p.m.
```

Readers report that right-justified is hard on the eye. The ragged right creates a softer, more natural look. Most published books are set up with justified margins, but that's for printed material, not everyday business correspondence.

(10) What I didn't include here because of the brevity of this memo are *headers*. Headers, equivalent to subheads in a newspaper, divide long memos into shorter topics. They break up lengthy text, show the reader what topic follows, provide easy reference for later use, and give visual variety to the page. Use judgment with headers, but if your memo's appearance and content improve with them, go ahead. Here's how:

MEMO

To: All Center Personnel
From: Shirley Sachs
Date: September 26,19XX
Subject: REPLACEMENT OF CONVENIENCE COPIERS

NEW EQUIPMENT

During the week of September 28, the Center's
copiers will be replaced with new ABC equipment.
This change will improve copy quality and machine
dependability. In some cases, machine features will
be upgraded.

SEVEN-DIGIT USER NUMBER

To use the copiers, you must have a seven-digit user
number. With this number, we will be able to
regulate the number of copies each S/B department
employee makes. Your department secretary will
provide you with your user number.

USER NUMBER LIMITATIONS

Only copiers in your work area will accept your user
number. If you must use a different copier, consult
your department head for a universal user number.

EMERGENCY MEASURES

In case of a malfunction, there is a single
emergency number available for each copier. Restrict
this use to situations when no other copier works.

MEETING PLANNED

We'll hold a meeting on Monday, September 5 at 3:30
p.m. in the Conference Room to discuss any further
changes or concerns.

SS: ce
cc: Allen Yarowsky
     Mike Shires
     Ross Rattray
     Pete Cesarini
     Christi Wellington

(11) Salutation and signature lines are not necessary in memos. Sometimes, however, the writer will initial the memo before it circulates to show approval of content.

(12) This line provides the initials (in upper case) of the writer followed by a colon and the initial (in lower case) of the typist.

(13) The abbreviation "cc" refers to "carbon copy." Of course in this new age of word processors, carbons are an endangered species. Nevertheless, the term shows who else, besides the primary recipients, will receive the memo. If the "To:" line (number (2) gives a general label such as, "All Managers," "All Volunteers," or "Computer Operators," then the "cc" designates specific names, first and last.

Now that you know the format, what about specific types of memos? You may not consciously realize it, but there are specific reasons for writing certain types of memos. They include *courtesy, follow-up, informative, confirmation,* and *directive.* Keeping these reasons in mind as you write helps you stick to your purpose.

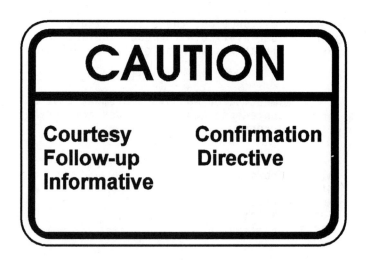

CAUTION

Courtesy   Confirmation
Follow-up   Directive
Informative

When do you use each one?

TYPE	REASON
courtesy	"thank you," "I appreciate," "let's do it again."
follow-up	"to answer your question," "I've researched the matter," "here's a follow-up."
informative	"to let you know," "here are the facts," "I'll be leaving Sunday."
confirmation	"thank you for the shipment," "we got your letter," "we'll meet you in Los Angeles."
directive	"would you please," "pick me up," "be on time."

But if these formats leave you still wondering how you are going to structure your paragraphs, then use the following sentence sequence to lead you along.

FIVE SIMPLE SEQUENCES

1. The *cause-effect sequence* details certain forces, then the results which follow; or it describes conditions or events, then discusses the forces which caused them. For example, in a memo concerning your company's safety program, list the kinds of circumstances in which accidents have been most likely to occur in your organization, then afterward include events that have actually happened (either within or outside your organization). Here's how:

When Sam Williams accidentally unplugged the computer, a major crisis occurred, causing many aspects of our operation to fail. From the week of June 15-June 22, the following reports were delayed:

❏ Production

❏ Labor

❏ Inventory

❏ Payroll.

In addition, employee morale worsened. The effect on our overall production has been disastrous. But since we have restored everything, we should be back on schedule soon. Thank you all very much for your cooperation.

2. The *chronologic sequence* begins at a certain period or date and moves forward or backward in time. Whenever you use this method, your discussion preserves the exact order of the occurrences that have taken place. If, for instance, you're a graveyard shift supervisor whose manager wants a detailed description of occurrences in your work area in the early morning, the chronological sequence will work. Here's how:

```
On September 5,19XX, at 2:36 a.m., Sally Hammond
reported that three disks containing important
information were missing. Security checked the
locks on her office door and desk at 3:04 a.m. to
find no tampering. By 4:33 a.m. after Sally had
returned from an errand, someone replaced the
disks. Please, although all materials in this
building are the property of TSM, be considerate of
an individual's possessions. If you need to borrow
something, leave a courtesy note. Then we can avoid
all this hassle.
```

3. The *problem solving sequence*, one of the most popular means of paragraph arrangement, starts with a specific description on a particular problem, or problems. It finishes with a discussion of solutions to that problem, or problems.

Let's say you're a newly hired advertising executive, struggling to keep several key clients who were unhappy with your predecessor's performance. You're convinced you can clean up the mess this person made, but your boss isn't so sure. This is a situation in which a well-written memo with a problem-solution sequence will help. If you subsequently do the unpleasant job, your memo might make you a legend in your own agency. Here's an example:

> The deadline for publication of our brochure is one week away, and we are crammed for time. If we can get the brochure out by this deadline, there is a bonus in it for everyone! To get this out, please use my suggestions. (And if you have more, let me know!)
>
> ☐ Postpone all other correspondence.
>
> ☐ Delay work on anything due after next week.
>
> ☐ Return only pertinent calls.
>
> Let's work hard on this important project!

4. The *spatial sequence* is useful in fewer situations than are the previous three forms. You'll understand why as soon as you see how it works. Spatial sequence material systematically moves from bottom to top, center to outside, east to west, north to south. Space is the case. There are certain instances in which this sequence should obviously be your one and only choice. If you're a real estate broker who has just listed a prime piece of commercial property, you'll probably be eager to let your agents know all out the assets of the land and the building on it. What better way to describe it than spatially? If you're a middle-level manager who has to handle a transfer of your corporate offices to a fancy new facility, you'll probably hope that the movers put your fellow executives' heavy furniture, not to mention yours, exactly where you want it. How about a spatially arranged memo for the mover's crew chief to ensure the success of this endeavor? Here's an example:

```
The room is well organized. On the left are
bookshelves. On the left-hand side there is a column
of shelves, which extend halfway across the width of
the closet. The first shelf has paper products. The
next one down contains discs, and the shelf below
that one has desk supplies. To the right of this
column of shelves are meeting tables. Next to them
are desks and chairs.
```

5. The *special topical sequence*, like the spatial one, isn't as universally useful as are the first three. Nevertheless, it's necessary, often obligatory, to use the topical sequence when tradition dictates that you follow an inflexible format ("We've always done it this way"), or when you must plan to meet predictable objections or questions. Most organizations, for example, have well-established formats for meeting minutes and periodic reports. Numerous public agencies have hard-and-fast structures for information and policy memos that include such items as: issue statements; recommendations; and discussions, which could cover background, pro-and-con analysis, fiscal impact, and suggested action steps.

MOLDING YOUR MEMOS: FORMS OF SUPPORT

All right, you say, pen poised over paper. I'm ready!

Now you know how to brainstorm and how to build an organized structure with your brainstorms. But if you go with what you've got, and that alone, you're likely to wind up with a memo that reminds your readers of a house with its wooden framework erected, and nothing else. You need some insides: external and internal walls, windows, doors, insulation. Effective business writers call these "forms of support." There are five of them, just as there are five major forms of paragraph arrangement.

SUPPORT FOR YOUR FORM

1. The *analogy or comparison* points out similarities between something known to your readers and something possibly unknown. The comparison of a memo with a house in the previous paragraph is an analogy; furthermore, it's a *figurative* analogy, which compares something belonging to one class or order with that of another. The other type, the *literal* analogy, compares one member with another member of the same class. Here are some examples:

```
FIGURATIVE              LITERAL


stars with eyes         volume of a pool with the
                        volume of a lake
airplane with bird      apples with oranges
carpeting with grass    Honda with Mercedes
```

2. The *definition or explanation* is a concise exposition that either clarifies an obscure form or comments on how the parts of a whole come together. Its characteristics are accuracy and brevity. It ought to be reinforced by other forms of supports. Here's another example of a definition/explanation:

```
The new postal service dictionary has zip codes for
all areas and also lists post office locations.
```

3. The *example or illustration* is, quite simply, a storytelling device, something that actually occurred or could have happened. The analogy or comparison can be subdivided, and so can this form of support, into *factual* and *hypothetical*. The factual example describes a real, true event or experience. The hypothetical illustration narrates what could or might take place under certain circumstances. This book is full of both. Here are examples:

FACTUAL

The copy machine broke down on Monday, causing a major delay for mailings.

HYPOTHETICAL

If the copy machine breaks down, a major delay for mailings will result.

---

4. *Statistics* are numbers which are supposed to summarize a great deal of data, emphasizing present trends, and predicting future developments. In short, they are carefully selected and analyzed figures that show important facts in a numerical format. Watch out though: statistics have received well-deserved bad press recently because disreputable people have tried to manipulate them into proving shaky points. Avoid this "crime" in your business memos. If you are going to use statistics, make sure to cite their source. This adds credibility. Without the citation, who knows the importance of the statistics!

An executive from the Accounting Department compiled these statistics on the company's expenditures.

- ☐ 15% advertising
- ☐ 36% production/manufacturing/output
- ☐ 35% salaries, benefits
- ☐ 7% reinvestment
- ☐ 7% interest paid on debts

Let's analyze these costs and see how we can redistribute them.

---

5. *Testimony* cites the conclusions or opinions of experts. But that alone won't carry you without good organization and better support. If you're going to use testimony, you should be able to answer yes or no questions. First, is the individual whose words you're quoting actually an authority in the specific field to which you're applying? Second, will your memo's readers be inclined to accept and respect this person as an authority? For example:

```
Sally Weed, our local computer expert, stated that
an additional terminal would greatly increase our
productivity.
```

All of these forms of support lend credibility and stability to your writing. They tell your readers you're a sophisticated, powerful writer.

The Perfect MEMO!

5

WRITE IT

WESTROOTS RULES OF WRITING

- ☐ DECREASE SENTENCE LENGTH
- ☐ OMIT NEEDLESS WORDS
- ☐ AVOID STUFFY LANGUAGE
- ☐ USE STRONG VERBS

So, now you've done your groundwork. It's almost time either to pick up the pen, use the dictation equipment, or fire up your word processor. Or perhaps you'll "ghostwrite" for someone else.

In truth, a great deal of business writing is done by somebody other than the person whose name appears at the bottom of the page. Why? Often the people at the top, the ones who sign the memo, are too busy to write or aren't confident of their writing skills. So, they pass the pen.

That pen gets passed at you, and you have to write a memo immediately. The responsibility is yours now. Here's how:

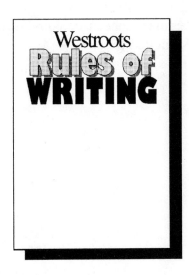

BACK TO BASICS: DISCOVERING AND APPLYING WESTROOTS RULES OF WRITING

Once you've decided on your content, Westroots Rules of Writing revolutionize the way you express it. These rules apply not only to memos, but also to letters, proposals, reports, and other documents. Here they are, the four keys to turning your sentences into direct, dynamic statements with power and purpose.

Westroots Rules will greatly improve your writing. Simply decrease sentence length, omit needless words, avoid stuffy language, and use strong verbs. Applying these rules is painless; you can do it too!

One reason people use longer written responses (over oral ones) is that they have time to consider their answers and are therefore able to explain in fuller detail. And oral responses usually include nonverbal enhancers (hand motions, voice tonality) that are absent in written communications. Most people try to "fill in" those missing enhancers when writing; perhaps some are better at it than others. But if you form your sentences powerfully and punctuate them correctly, your writing will be as memorable and concise as the finest speech or conversation you will ever deliver or be lucky enough to hear.

RULE 1: DECREASE SENTENCE LENGTH

Stop. Before you do anything else, go back to what you last wrote. Count the number of words in an average sentence. What number did you get?

- ☐ 20?

- ☐ 15?

- ☐ 25?

- ☐ 10?

- ☐ 30?

If you wanted to lower your blood pressure, you'd need a baseline figure to work from. The same goes for sentence length. In order to cut down the length, you have to know how your sentences are running. Are they over 20 words, all one length, all one style? If so, notice the patterns and begin to change them. The strongest sentences are under 20 words, varied in length, varied in style. Once you spot your patterns, you'll be able to change them.

Most people never consider how many words they customarily use. It doesn't matter much, you may say. On the contrary, it could be of critical importance to your writing. Besides, you were trained in school that "longer is better," so you have been using as many words as you can to round out your sentences and fill up your pages.

Psychologically, people don't like to read long sentences. Do you? Recall the most recent thing you read that had any impact. It probably wasn't lengthy. It probably didn't fill up one page and spill over onto another. Neither should your writing.

There's no golden rule to regulate how many words should be in a sentence. Research has shown that about 20 words is an average number for the reader to comprehend comfortably. If you go beyond, it's likely you're either repeating, adding redundant words or phrases, or splicing on a new idea. I recommend that you have an idea of how many words you write in an average sentence, then consciously try to limit your sentences to a length of from 17 to 20 words, at the most.

If right now you had to verbally describe what you do at your job, what would you say? You'd probably react to this request articulately and succinctly. You'd say, "I'm the department manager for my computer firm." Or, "I am a member of the nursing staff." Or, "I write the newsletters for my company." That's very straightforward. And yet, if I were to ask you to transform the same body of information into writing, what would happen?

Are you smiling? Probably, because at this point you're realizing that the 10 to 12 words you spoke would suddenly swell to 20 to 25. Why? Honest individuals admit that they expand their writing on paper to impress their readers with either their importance or their intelligence. Unfortunately, the outcome is often the opposite of what they had intended. Wordiness distances you from your readers. From the start, monitor the number of words you write in your sentences. See if you can keep them under control. To test for length, you can count the number of words and limit them. A sentence should run no longer than two lines on a typed page; this is another way to test effective sentence length. Less is fine. Finally, read your sentence aloud. If you have to take a second breath before finishing, your sentence is too long. So, give your sentences the count, eyeball, or breath test. If you fail any of these, rewrite and shorten your sentence.

Business writers also tend to use the same number of words in sentence after sentence. It's like listening to a speaker who has a monotone voice. It is boring to hear somebody whose pitch, rate, and volume never vary! Monotony can creep into and deaden writing the same way it does speaking. The antidote to this poison is simple: vary the number of words in your sentences. In fact, when you have a very important point to make, say it in a short sentence for impact and variety.

Here's a monotonous memo opening:

> Please make sure you come back from your lunch break on schedule. The schedule of your hours is posted in the Staff Room. Please let me know if you have special plans.

This paragraph is boring because all the sentences read in a basic pattern and run the same length. Spice up your sentences this way:

> Lunch schedules are important. Yours is posted in the Staff Room. It's important that you come back on time, but if you have special plans, please clear them with me before you leave the office.

"Okay," you might say, "how do I shorten my sentences? It's all very well to say I know I need to shorten them. How can I make that happen?" The good news is that you don't have to do a whole rewrite. Just shorten, break, and split your sentences. Here's how:

TIPS FOR SHORTER SENTENCES

- ☐ KEEP SENTENCES AROUND 20 WORDS:
- ☐ VARY SENTENCE LENGTH
- ☐ LIST WHENEVER YOU CAN

SPLIT THE SENTENCE. What does this mean? Tighten and shorten your sentences. Every long sentence is either two thoughts tacked together or one thought repeated in different words. A sentence contains one primary thought. Yet most writers use a single sentence to jam two disjointed ideas together. So when you monitor your sentences, pay attention to your tendency to do this. Gustave Flaubert said, "Whenever you can shorten a sentence, do. And one always can. The best sentence? The shortest." Take this sentence, for example:

```
In 19XX, then corporate vice president Steven
Fromm, a dynamic Speaker and organizer, established
a new company, the Brown Organization, and
persuaded a number of supervisors and managers to
come to work for him.
```

This sentence is accurate, and it certainly contains necessary information. But it's long and awkward. Where would you split it? You'll notice immediately that the natural breaking point is after the word "Organization." Simply put a period after the word "Organization," strike out the word "and," and add "He." What you have left is two shorter, tighter sentences closely linked, yet two units that are much more readable than the original.

Remember this guideline: look for the "and" and break before it. Frequently, people use the word "and" to say "chocolate and vanilla," connecting two themes. That's fine. But it's not fine when you're connecting two major complete ideas to bridge one sentence to the next. Spot the "and" and break before it. Put a period before the "and," capitalize the first word in the next sentence, and then go on with your new sentence. The result is two tight sentences instead of one loose, rambling one. The difference is startling.

Here's another sentence:

> Every attempt was made to verify Mr. Smith's
> insurance, and I have attached for your information
> a written narrative of all the events that took
> place in our attempt to do this.

Again, there are two thoughts stuffed into one lengthy unit. So, spot the "and" and break before it:

> Every attempt was made to verify Mr. Smith's
> insurance. I have attached for your information a
> written narrative of all the events that took place
> in our attempt to do this.

Here you have two shorter, tighter sentences. You keep your reader engaged. Furthermore, you add variety in sentence length, which is desirable.

TAKE CARE WITH CONNECTIVES. Writers unconsciously hook two ideas together with a connecting word instead of stopping the sentence, by starting with an introductory connective and continuing. The writer of the following memo wanted to pass the word to all members of his organization that he had been promoted:

> It is with mixed emotions that I leave the Eastgate
> facility, however, I am looking forward to my new
> endeavor with a great deal of enthusiasm and
> optimism, and you may be assured that I will do
> everything possible to continue building the
> Eastgate facility.

That's a mouthful to say. In fact, it's also an eyeful for any reader.

What's your response to this writing? Probably to back off and remark, "Wow, I can barely get through that block of verbiage!" And that's how readers feel when they're confronted with writing that's more than two lines of a typed page. It's too long.

For starters, break the sentence before the word "however." "However" is a transition word or a connective: connectives are gold. They show your reader that you're moving smoothly from one thought to the next. They also indicate relationships between ideas. The Appendix includes a list of connectives for your convenience.

On the bulletin board above my desk, I've tacked up a list of connectives that help me keep my sentences from becoming too choppy or too broken up. When I need to glide smoothly from one thought into the next, I glance up at my list to pick the correct connective. "However," is popular; others include "moreover," "nevertheless," and "consequently." See the Appendix for a more complete list.

At the same time that I suggest you use connectives, I also want to warn you about them. Some writers become so fascinated by them that they try to stick them into every single sentence, which is obviously too much. I also urge you to try to move away from the more formal connectives: replace "however" with "but," "consequently" with "so," and "moreover" with "now." The shift in today's business writing is from formal to informal. Your well-tuned ear will let you know when it's appropriate to follow.

If you're unfamiliar with connectives or transition words, begin to play around with them as a way to prevent your short sentences from becoming too choppy. Also, if you're going to use your connectives to start sentences, end the sentence before the connective, then begin the new sentence with your connective. Here's an example:

> I'd like a new position. But, I've only worked here three months and don't have much experience.

Rather than having one rambling, extended sentence, the writer now has two concise, smoothly connected sentences. The shift might not seem big, but look at it and listen to the difference. It is a direct way of writing.

SAMPLE SENTENCES

☐ Charts are analyzed and coded in a timely fashion and sent on to doctor's files for completion within a few days of discharge which helps decrease delinquent charts.

☐ Because of the complexities of the situation I have decided to pay the full assessment on the property and consequently I have directed the Board of Governors to begin proceedings to provide the Seal Company with adequate funds to cover this initial expense.

☐ If this method of operation is to continue it does raise the issue of why we are marketing a similar product abroad, however, we could discuss it further in Washington, D.C., at our annual meeting.

Now, break them up:

- ☐ Charts are analyzed and coded in a timely fashion. They're sent to doctor's files for completion within a few days of discharge. This procedure helps decrease delinquent charts.

- ☐ Because of the complexities of the situation, I have decided to pay the full assessment on the property. Consequently, I have directed the Board of Governors to begin proceedings. This process will provide the Seal Company with adequate funds to cover this initial expense.

- ☐ If this method of operation is to continue, it does't . raise the issue of why we are marketing a similar product abroad. However, we could discuss it further in Washington, D.C., at our annual meeting.

WRITE WITH WHITE. When you first pick up a letter, what's your reaction? Too long? Too hard on the eye? No breaks? Writing is as much a visual as an auditory and intellectual experience. The way your words look on the page matters just as much as the way they sound when you read them. You might wonder, "What do looks have to do with this? Writing's nothing like dressing." But believe me, it is. When you see a piece of paper, your first reaction is not to what you read. Your response is to what you see. It's like an initial meeting with someone. Sure, you're interested in what that individual has to say and what sort of person she is, but you're also impressed by what you see. Look at these memos:

NO WHITE SPACE:

MEMO

To: Sales Associates
From: Vicki Fuller
Date: May 9, 19XX
Subject: ERRORS & OMISSIONS

Your Errors & Omissions insurance contribution was
due February 28. Please give your $1,000 check to
Patty today or she will begin deductions from your
next commission check. We are waiting for the E & O
insurance quote from Mick S. Shires Company. As soon
as they answer, we will let you know.

Thanks!

vf

cc: Leanne Wills
      James Zarro
      Caroline Bach
      Patty Le Wallen

WHITE SPACE:

MEMO

To: John Brown
From: Mary Van Pelt
Date: April 15, 19XX
Subject: EXPIRED LISTINGS

While examining my files, I ran across some expired listings. They are:

2376-2388 Via Milla Street   expired April 1
2393 Via Milla Street   expired February 3

Updated listings let you receive your commission checks. Please let me know *ASAP* about your status. If you have any current listings, let me know.

Thanks!

ml
cc: Jerry Fredd
     Suzi White
     Bill Bloomfield

Let's face it, though: appearances are important.

This fact applies to writing as well. The way your words look on a page has a great deal to do with whether they draw your readers in or shut them out. You may ask, "What can I do to make my writing more visually appealing?" exactly as you might ask an image consultant, "What can I do to make my physical appearance more appealing?" (No, you don't want to write on day-glo paper with neon ink—that's not the type of attention you're after.)

Creating "white space" on the page is a subtle yet powerful method of producing a positive impression for your readers. What is white space? When you look at a page, you see blocks of type broken by white space.

What does all this white space do? Something surprisingly strange: it rests our readers' eyes, invites them in and motivates them to read over your memo thoroughly. Instead of overwhelming them with a large block of type, you break the memo up into manageable chunks of material, giving the readers room to move right along through what you've written, digesting it as they go.

Creating white space by listing has been around for a long time and is sure to stay. Why? Because it's a great way to get your ideas on paper in an efficient, effective, and easy-to-read format. I once received a memo from a large computer transportation company that wanted me to do a seminar for them. When I was going to be interviewed, they sent me a preliminary letter. The sophisticated writer knew exactly how to present her material, using plenty of white space. She listed each of the items I was to bring for the interview. The night before the meeting, I quickly scanned her list and checked off each item as I prepared for the meeting. Had the letter been disorganized, I would have been too!

Clean memos demand attention. With a perfect memo, things will be done correctly—the first time! So, when you write a memo, be aware of how it looks. For example, you may have a complex sentence that's full of information. Maybe you've just come back from a meeting; you want to let your supervisors or subordinates know what you learned. Your initial inclination is to write a sentence something like this:

```
The purpose of the workshop was to discuss state,
local, and federal water quality regulations, the
economic impact of waste control, and concepts and
methods of monitoring wastes.
```

You've said precisely what the purpose of the meeting was, and you've expressed it with correct grammar and punctuation.

Look at the sentence a little more closely—what do you see? Let me tell you what I see: a block of type and a series of technical words stacked on top of each other. If I'm extremely motivated, I'll muddle through, but it isn't inviting. You can write this same sentence more attractively without compromising its meaning. Set it up this way:

```
The purpose of the workshop was to discuss:

□ Federal, state, and local water quality
  regulations

□ The economic impact of waste control

□ Concepts and methods of monitoring wastes.
```

What do these changes accomplish? Everything! You've drawn attention to the three main subjects discussed at the workshop. Instead of burying them in an extended sentence, you've separated them so that they stand out. By indenting the individual items and placing clean-looking bullets in front of them, you've used white space to put your reader's attention where you want it. Bullets can be any symbol—they can be *, ●, —. However, I prefer the bullet ●. Most computers can't print this symbol, so use the small "o" and fill it in—if you have a steady hand. My second preference is the dash: it's clean and easy to recognize. Asterisks are too "glitzy." They call attention to the mark, not the words. By using symbols, you catch your reader's eye and give more impact to your point. You may be wondering, "What about numbering my points?" That's the way you were taught in school, but in modern business writing, people prefer bullets. Why? Because numbers, or letters, prioritize your points. Generally, listed items are not written for order of importance, so leave the numbers out. Use the bullets. If, however, you do want to designate priority, then use numbers.

Here's another sentence. You'd like to list your goals for the new year:

> Therefore, the following goals for 1993-94 accomplish these developmental needs of an effective marketing program. We want to establish a functional marketing framework, make a profitable, comprehensive profit and loss program, establish a customer satisfaction program, and develop an ongoing marketing audit of our share and growth program.

The grammar and punctuation are correct, but can the reader comprehend it? No! You've lessened the impact of the sentence. Listing your items gives them priority.

Here's the same sentence presented in a list form:

> Therefore the 1993-94 goals accomplish these developmental needs of an effective marketing program:
>
> ❏ Establishing a functional marketing framework
>
> ❏ Developing a profitable, comprehensive program
>
> ❏ Making a customer satisfaction program
>
> ❏ Creating an ongoing marketing audit of our share and growth program.

You put white space on the page, highlight your elements, make them important, and create readability.

HOW TO PERFECT YOUR LISTS. A bank employee composed the next list. Analyze what he has attempted to do.

```
The status information immediately informs us of: a)
Is it a statement or is it a passbook? b) is the
account open or is it closed? c) effective date of
account opened? d) prior transaction e) statement
cycle f) interest pay cycle.
```

The writer has itemized the status information: But the list is written in nonparallel form. You might ask, "What's parallel form?" Good question! Although listing is a very simple and powerful way to write, for you to do it well, I advise that you follow some guidelines.

One guideline is, *write your list in parallel form.* Look at the first sample sentence in this section:

```
The purpose of the workshop was to discuss state,
local, and federal water quality regulations, the
economic impact of waste control, and concepts and
methods of monitoring wastes
```

Those items as listed are all in parallel form; they are items in a series, all listed in the same part of speech, in approximately the same length, and in a similar format. The same format works for the second sample sentence. Each item starts with the word "to" and is followed by a verb: "establish," "develop," "make," and "present"; these are four infinitives, easy-to-read, easy-to-follow, and in parallel form.

The problem with the last sample list is that the writer starts out with two questions: "Is it a statement or is it a passbook?" and "is the account open or is it closed?" and then shifts to a series of fragments rather than questions. This shift breaks the train of thought and the chain of concentration, setting a jarring rather than pleasant reading experience.

You can turn those final three items to questions or turn all into a parallel format to make the list retain the same content. Here's how. Keep the first two items similar: "Is it a statement or is it a passbook?"; keep the second one, "is the account open or is it closed?"; and make the third one "what was the effective date the account was opened, what was the account balance, what was the interest date, and what was the interest pay cycle?" That phrasing puts all your items in a parallel, question format which makes them easier to read. Look at the following three sentences containing items in a series, and see if you can turn them into lists.

```
I would appreciate your cooperation with the
following procedures for ordering and using
audiovisual equipment and supplies: (1) place all
orders directly with the Audiovisual Department, NOT
through the Center Directors; (2) you MUST notify us
AT LEAST seven working days before use; (3) pick up
AND RETURN all audiovisual equipment and supplies at
the Center Director's desk so that others may use
materials as needed.

This system will help enhance our service by freeing
up ticket counter and gate lines, allowing more
personal attention for those passengers needing out-
of-the-ordinary assistance, maximizing our service
while keeping costs low, and offering 24-hour check-
in service.

Membership on a monitoring team would require the
person to commit to three to four days' time, and to
serve on the monitoring team for a school site
designated for monitoring, 1993-1994.
```

How do your answers compare?

I would appreciate your cooperation with the following procedures for ordering and using audiovisual equipment and supplies:

- ☐ Place all orders directly with the Audiovisual Department, NOT through the Center Directors.

- ☐ Notify us AT LEAST seven working days before use.

- ☐ Pick up AND RETURN all audiovisual equipment and supplies at the Center Director's desk so that others may use materials as needed.

This system will help enhance our service by:

- ☐ Freeing up ticket counter and gate lines

- ☐ Allowing more personal attention for those passengers needing out-of-the-ordinary assistance

- ☐ Maximizing our service while keeping costs low, and offering 24-hour check-in service.

Membership on a monitoring team would require the person to:

- ☐ Commit to three to four days' time

- ☐ Serve on the monitoring team for a school site designated for monitoring, 1993-1994.

LISTING IN PARALLEL FORM

- ☐ KEEP LISTS BRIEF
- ☐ BEGIN WITH VERBS WHERE POSSIBLE
- ☐ WATCH TENSES AND FORMS
- ☐ LIMIT SUBLISTS
- ☐ STATE THREE TO FIVE POINTS ONLY

ROUNDING OUT YOUR LISTS. Now you know the basics of how to list your items. Can you think of a memo you wrote recently at work, one in which you hadn't inserted a list, but later wished you had? Most readers and writers who discover this technique immediately jump on it as a most effective, efficient, and powerful way of developing and enhancing their writing skills.

Nevertheless, a client once called me to say, "Pat, that's a terrific technique you taught my employees. The trouble with it is that now they want to list anything and everything!" A little caution I'd like to throw your way is this: certainly, listing is powerful and effective, but as with your transitions, don't overdo it. If you list every single item in your memo, you may wind up with a laundry list instead of well-written material.

One final footnote to lists: instead of ending your paragraph with the last listed item, you can round it out with a sentence that will summarize the significance of the list itself.

Go back to the first sentence you worked with in the section "The purpose of the workshop was to discuss...." After you've listed that last item, instead of plunging into the next paragraph, which might unbalance your page, you can complement your list with a capsule sentence. For example, you might say at the end of the list, "Fifteen people attended the workshop." That way you have sandwiched your list between one opening and one closing sentence, set off the items you want to list, and created a very visually appealing page. Now you're ready to go into your next paragraph, which probably will not contain a list.

MORE WAYS TO CREATE WHITE SPACE. Although I'm not a great believer in breaking up sentences unnecessarily in the middle, there are times when inserting dashes internally in an item will both highlight it and create white space. Look at the following example and see how this technique works. Say you have a sentence that reads,

```
Other companies—including Intron in New York City—
are much more flexible than our Bicorp Company in
San Diego.
```

Does it seem as if there's not much difference? Indeed there isn't. But those little dashes do a lot to create some white space on the page. It's a small technicality, but visually it does well. Another method to create space on the page is to put in parentheses an item in the middle of your sentence. I'm not talking about an abbreviation; I'm referring to a sentence that probably could contain some information in parenthetical punctuation. Consider the following:

```
As Pittsburgh Production Company's prices change
(either for manufactured materials or for storage),
a corresponding decrease in profit could occur if
these increases are not covered by our own
increases.
```

Having given you those two options for creating more white space, I'm going to add a major caution about them. Don't break up the flow of a sentence unnecessarily. While I've suggested that dashes might highlight the information you want to put inside the sentence, parentheses are a different matter. I tend to think that parentheses break up the flow of an other wise smoothly written sentence, sometimes creating more difficulty than clarity for your readers. So I caution you about parenthetical information. Here's an example of a writer who uses parentheses in the middle of a sentence to try to get a break in the flow of her writing. Unfortunately, she creates more chaos than clarity.

```
Most sophisticated PC users recognize that off-line
systems are only marginally appropriate for personal
computers (see attached copy of an article from PC
Week, April 3, 19XX, page 6, for a discussion of the
inappropriateness of the Old Reliable (OR) standby
systems for use with an IBM PC . . . OR is the
largest manufacturer of standby systems), and in no
case adequate if a modem is in use.
```

Unless you have a good reason for breaking up the flow of a sentence with parentheses, try not to do it. Dashes are another story; used in moderation, they're fine. Sometimes writers like to break up the flow of a sentence and create some white space by putting a colon within the sentence itself. Here is an example:

```
There are presently three supermarkets supplying
Orlando: The Superstore, Price Right, and Good Buy.
```

By putting the colon in the middle of that sentence, you indicate to your reader that a list will follow. You have also created some white space: the space before the colon, the colon itself, and the space after it.

Therefore, you have four separate ways of creating white space within the sentence itself. In review, they are:

☐ Items in a list beneath the sentence

☐ Dashes within the sentence

☐ Parentheses within the sentence

☐ Colons within the sentence.

Several other ways exist to create white space on the page, and I urge you to consider them when you write. When you look at paragraphs on a page in a lengthy memo, they usually provide no visual break for readers. There is a way to do it, however, and with hardly any trouble to you.

Notice the way this book is set up. You have frequent breaks in each section. I've done that with subheads. They're a useful way to break up material, leading your reader from one topic to the next without breaking the continuity from one section to the next. Subheads create white space on the page. Each time you break a section, you have white space before your subhead, then the subhead itself, followed by the next section. Here's an example:

MEMO

To: Lois Gartella
From: Mike Foley
Date: May 22,19XX
Subject: NEW BIDS FOR THE WAREHOUSE ROOF

PATCHING ROOF

Four roofers have submitted bids to repair the
warehouse roof. The lowest bidder suggests patching
rather than redoing the entire roof.

REPAIRING ROOF

Others disagree with this bidder. They point out
that the roof has already been patched too many
times. It needs to be overhauled and have heat
sealed polymer sheets applied.

DECISION

I agree with the other bidders. Polymer roofing
comes with a 20-year guarantee compared to 2 years.
Since we desperately need a warehouse, I suggest we
give the contract to the lowest bidder of the
polymer system.

MEETING

Let's have a meeting next Tuesday at 3:15 p.m. in
the lounge to discuss this decision. Thanks!

There's nothing more distancing to your reader than writing one long paragraph after another. A solid block of type is hard on the eyes and the senses. Consequently, just as I've cautioned you in the beginning of this section to decrease your sentence length, I also encourage you to decrease your paragraph length.

How many sentences per paragraph? Again, there's no golden rule. But any paragraph of more than five sentences probably spills into more than one topic. And back to what your teachers taught: the purpose of a paragraph is to present one idea and one idea only. So write your paragraph topic sentence, go into a brief explanation—possibly an example—then stop, move into your next paragraph indicated by a transition or subhead, and you're on your way.

These are the top tools for shortening sentences. In turn, they will shorten your paragraphs.

☐ Reduce the number of words.

☐ Break two sentences from one long one.

☐ Separate with punctuation marks.

☐ Create valuable, priceless white space on the page.

☐ Write clever subheads.

☐ Keep your paragraphs short.

These guidelines create positive, powerful responses in your reader's mind. Your writing is stronger already!

RULE 2: OMIT NEEDLESS WORDS

Many people think that better writing requires them to reformulate and restate entire phrases, sentences, and paragraphs. Again, in school we were taught to redo, rework, rephrase, restate. Longer was better. That's not the case at all! Often editing merely involves cutting out, not a complete rewriting.

Cutting is like working with scissors. If you've written a phrase or sentence and you've gone back to revise it, there may be many extra words that you don't need. Take this example:

```
There is no doubt but that we need to make changes
in our company.
```

The sentence is grammatically acceptable; too bad it's wordy and contains unnecessary phrases. "There is no doubt but that" is awkward and lengthy to digest. You could just as easily write,

```
Doubtless we need to make some changes in our
company.
```

or

```
We need to make changes in our company.
```

While we're on this subject, look at the first two words, "There is." "There is," "there are," "there was," and "there were," are called expletive constructions. Expletives are extras. These words automatically start wasted expressions that will never enhance or energize your composition. As you write, get rid of these useless introductions. You want to begin with power. It's those first words that make the most memorable impression. Listen to one more sentence with wasted words:

```
He is a man who works for Crown Corporation.
```

"He is a man who": which words could you cut? What about "is a man who"? Again, extra words. Just say,

```
He works for Crown Corporation.
```

Those are the essential words in that sentence. No others need to stay.

Remember, the purpose of your memo is to state your message briefly. Extra words delay your impact and power. A sentence should contain only necessary words. "Is a man who" contains unnecessary words; delete them and you're on your way to a much more effective sentence.

Another example:

```
In a hasty manner, I finished my work.
```

You could shorten the whole thing by saying, "Hastily, I finished my work." "Hastily" is more visually compact and verbally powerful .

How about "the fact that you asked me makes me want to give my opinion"? "The fact that" is an awkward construction. (In a few minutes it'll be time to talk about writing things the way you would say them.) Lots of people start their sentences with "the fact that," yet none of those three words has any real charge. If you could measure them with a verbal Geiger Counter, would any of them register over 1 or 2? I don't think so. Why don't you make a resolution that you're not going to choose any words that register under 4 on this kind of counter (well, maybe 3)?

How about another one: "This is a subject that interests me." "Is a subject that": if you ran your Geiger counter over that phrase, the only word that would register anything reasonable would probably be "subject." "Is," for instance, weakens the verb. So why not cut out the other words? "This subject interests me" becomes a far more powerful sentence than its predecessor.

Banks have made many changes, but in many cases they still hold onto wordy constructions and archaic jargon. For instance, "I wrote a check in the amount of $49.20" could be cut to "I wrote a check for $49.20."

So cut out extras—those words that get low readings on your Geiger counter. They contribute nothing significant to the literary force of your sentence, and they delay the delivery of your message.

The senior trainer for a large bank assembled her new employees at their downtown branch for a demonstration on how to take customer deposits. An elderly gentleman walked to the window with a complicated transaction. In her most long-winded "bankingese" she told him how to fill out his slips and complete the transaction. He listened attentively, but moments later he looked up at her and said, "I don't understand one word you just said." Embarrassed, she recognized the problem. She cut her explanation in half, simplified her language, and got her point across much more successfully.

Both she and her trainees learned a lot that day.

PREPPING YOUR PREPOSITIONS. This next sentence includes another grammatically interesting situation:

```
A colleague of mine called yesterday.
```

The expression "of mine" is what grammarians call a prepositional phrase. Take that prepositional phrase and try this trick. Circle "of mine," change it into a one-word adjective, and substitute for "a colleague" so that the sentence says,

```
My colleague called yesterday.
```

See how that works?

If you're writing a memo to someone who's recently written you one, you might start with the sentence,

```
A memo from you arrived on my desk yesterday.
```

Why not tighten it up to read,

```
Your memo arrived yesterday.
```

It's an improvement for more than one reason: you are spotlighting your reader instead of yourself. Everyone enjoys reading a memo with "you" or "your" rather than "I" or "my." It's a subtle way to win people over with your writing. Remember to adopt the "you" attitude.

Where can you cut the fat out of the following sentence?

```
Below are provided general guidelines which should
be followed for review purposes.
```

Often writers dilute the strength of their sentences by starting with empty words like the expletive "there is." They also try to tack on extra words at the end. Does the word "purposes" mean anything much in this sentence? Not really. Why not conclude with the word "review"? "Purposes," I'd relegate to the category of empty words. Lots of empty words like "purposes" fill people's writing. Just write:

```
Below are guidelines for review.
```

More appear in the Appendix for your reference.

CUT OUT CLICHÉS. You can also cut out empty words and phrases by eliminating clichés. What exactly is a cliché? It's an old, outdated, overused phrase or expression that's been around forever. Since you didn't create the phrase, it isn't yours. For example, common clichés from everyday communication include:

☐ "as far as the eye can see"

☐ "blind as a bat"

☐ "dead as a doornail"

☐ "it's old hat"

☐ "we don't see eye to eye on the issue"

☐ "please don't hesitate to call"

☐ "when in doubt, leave it out."

For instance, you may say in a memo, "it might be old hat to you, but let's review the company policy on tardiness." The trouble is that "it's old hat" isn't new with you, and it's not a unique way of speaking to your readers. They've heard it before.

Originality and personality are keys to effective business writing. When you use somebody else's business writing words, you aren't giving the best of yourself. Other clichés to avoid include:

☐ "last but not least"

☐ "in the final analysis"

☐ "in actual fact."

They have lost their punch through overuse, and they certainly don't convey your individual character or insight. Rely on your spoken voice to phrase your words—they'll be a lot more "you"!

OVERDOING THE OBVIOUS. Something else that you can easily cut out is a category I call "excessive explanation of the obvious." Writers often begin their sentences by warming up like a baseball pitcher. In the process, they lose the words that are guaranteed to grab their readers' attention. Good examples are phrases such as these:

☐ "that is to say"

☐ "in other words"

☐ "to repeat myself."

I advise you to avoid them altogether. If you've said something in other words, or you've already said it clearly, you don't need other words to say it again. Or instead of starting your sentences with "that is to say," just go ahead and get it out. Writers also begin with "as you already know." If your audience members already know it, don't insult their intelligence by telling them again.

Another category of detail that delays or impedes clarity is unnecessary modifiers, also known as redundancies. These are phrases like:

- ☐ "loud clamor"

- ☐ "pointed peak"

- ☐ "empty vacuum"

or that Madison Avenue favorite

- ☐ "a most unique product."

(If it's "unique," you know it's "most.") Redundant phrases feature repetition or excessive explanation, both unnecessary in business writing. The Appendix includes additional redundant phrases.

But what about repetition to reinforce an idea? Some people think that repeating certain statements gets the idea across more strongly. Repetition is no compliment to your reader's intellect, particularly in memos. If you said it clearly the first time, there's no need to go over it again. Repetition might be fine for an advertisement, but not for a memo. Spare yourself, and your audience; say it clearly and effectively one time only.

Another category that often inflates memos is irrelevant detail. That's the last thing you want; it detracts from your central concept. Stick to the kinds of relevant items we've discussed in previous sections.

An excerpt from a repetitive memo:

```
An additional statement will be added to the report.
```

If you know the statement will be added, you know it will be additional, right? Keep your sentences as short and as tight as you possibly can. By eliminating unnecessary repetition, you get right to the point and powerfully.

Another example of extra words:

```
During the course of study, the research team
gathered some opinions for further consideration.
```

Pick out the extra words the writer has put in. Did you get this?

```
During the study, the survey team gathered opinions
for consideration.
```

"Study" by definition has "the course" built into it. "Some" and "for consideration" are equally nonessential. One more:

```
Notify the supervisors of any typing to be required
between the hours of 4:00 and 6:00 p.m.
```

It's obvious that 4:00 and 6:00 are hours because they're followed by "p.m." There's no need for "the hours of."

```
Notify the supervisors between 4:00 and 6:00 p.m. of
any typing you need.
```

or

```
Notify the supervisors of typing to be done between
4 and 6 p.m.
```

Tighten the sentence and you'll have taken off a lot of padding.

Instead of providing important information, many writers like to flaunt their egos at the beginning of their memos. Here's one who did exactly that:

```
In my opinion, I think there is a good chance they
will respond to our offer.
```

If you think it, it's evident that it's your opinion, and "in my opinion" is an egotistical and inefficient way to get going. Why not just begin with:

```
I think they will respond to our offer.
```

Then you can support your opinion in the next part of the sentence .

```
I think there is a good chance they will respond to
our offer to purchase two acres on the northeast
corner of South Street.
```

It includes only necessary information, says what you need to say, and puts your readers (rather than you) in the forefront. That's precisely what you want to do with your business writing.

Cut out extras: words, phrases, ideas, and information not absolutely essential to your memo's efficiency and effect. Go with these guidelines to get to what really matters. Make your writing as efficient as your work.

OMIT NEEDLESS WORDS

☐ "WIND-UP" WORDS
☐ EMPTY WORDS, PHRASES
☐ REDUNDANCIES
☐ CLICHÉS
☐ EXPLETIVES
☐ REPETITION

RULE 3: AVOID STUFFY LANGUAGE

This rule is the cornerstone of the SPEAKWRITE method. If you relax your stuffy language, your memos will sound as if they were written by a natural, congenial person, instead of a pompous, pretentious person. Here's a short list of examples.

LONGWINDED VS.	STRAIGHTFORWARD
In order to	To
Ten a.m. in the morning	10 a.m.
In view of	Because or Since
In the event of	If
Prior to	Before
With reference to	About (or leave out)
With regard to	About (or leave out)
Upon that date	On that date
At that point in time	Then
At this point in time	Now
Past experience	Experience

Would you say, "Prior to coming to work this morning, I made three phone calls"? If you did, I think your colleagues would stare at you and probably with good reason. No, you'd say, "Before coming to work this morning...." If you speak it that way, why don't you write it similarly? Look at some sentences and see how the SPEAKWRITE method would relax them:

```
It is necessary that the material be received in
this office by June 10.
```

"It is" is a lengthy way of beginning your sentence, and "be received" is awkward as well. Just say,

```
We need the material by June 10.
```

or

```
The material must reach us by June 10.
```

It's also a good idea in the SPEAKWRITE way of writing to meet your reader's need, not that of your own ego. Most writing is self-centered, starting with the pronouns "I" and "we." Why not highlight your reader instead of yourself, and use "you" and "your" more frequently? For example, instead of writing,

```
I would like to extend my congratulations for a job
well done.
```

say,

```
Congratulations on the job you did.
```

or

> Congratulations on your excellent work.

That highlights the person who did the job, not your congratulations to them.

Read the way a group of readers was addressed:

> It is requested that all personnel planning to take leave in December fill in the enclosed schedule.

If you received this kind of memo, you'd probably feel very depersonalized and disregarded; I know I would. Why not write a memo that talks directly to your audience?

> If you plan to take leave in December, please fill in the enclosed schedule.

RELY ON EVERYDAY WORDS. The complexity of business and the need for precision do require some big words, but don't use other big words when little ones will do. People who speak in small words often let big ones burden their writing. For example, you might say the word "help," but you write "assistance." You might say "pay," yet write "remuneration." You might say "visit," and write "visitation." These are inflated, overdressed words. Here are some more. Instead of saying "start," you write "commence," "help" becomes "facilitate," "best" turns to "optimum," "use" to "utilize." Some people call these words "businessese" or "corporatese." Whatever you call them, they don't work well in business writing.

Read the following memo. Imagine it's 4 p.m. on a Thursday. You're busy, tired, and overworked. What's your response (visually, intellectually, and emotionally)?

```
To:       Management Support
From:     Deposit Operations
Date:     June 14,19XX
Subject:  EMPLOYEE SUGGESTIONS

Attached please find an Employee Suggestion Form
which was sent to our area for review and comment.
Based upon input from Legal, Mail Services, Item
Processing, Credit Cards and Investment Support, we
feel that implementation of this suggestion would
not be feasible at this time. The major concern
regarding the suggestion came from the Legal
Department. They felt that if this were implemented,
it would have to be done on a selective basis by
employees due to the possibility of exposing
confidential information.
```

Compare it to:

```
To:       Management Support
From:     Tim Zimsi
Date:     June 14,19XX
Subject:  EMPLOYEE SUGGESTIONS

We can't use this suggestion now. Our legal, mail
services, item processing, credit cards, and
investment support people thought it wouldn't be
possible.

The legal department had the major concern. They
felt that if we used the suggestion, it would have
to be done selectively. They're worried about
exposing confidential information.
```

To give variety and interest to what you have to say, mix your sentence length as you would when speaking. Limit your sentences to twenty words. There is an eye test for your sentence length; if it runs over two typed lines, it's too long. There's an ear test as well: read your writing out loud. If you have to take more than one breath, your sentence is too long. (It's true in speaking, too.) If you have to breathe in the middle of a sentence, you're probably boring or inundating your listeners with too much talk.

Look for opportunities to reach out to your reader. Ask more questions. Instead of saying,

> Please notify this department as to whether the conference has been rescheduled,

why not just say,

> Has the conference been rescheduled?

Questions engage your reader's attention and interest, bringing them closer to you. Lazy writing overuses vague terms and uses weak adjectives. Look at these phrases: "Immense dedication," "enhanced programs," "viable hardware." Such broad terms don't communicate specifics. Just reading those terms, do you have any notion of what they really mean? I don't think so. The writers are trying to puff themselves up into a more professional image. Instead, they sound quite pompous and hard to understand. Use concrete examples rather than abstract adjectives to communicate more effectively and efficiently to your reader.

WRITE TO EXPRESS, NOT TO IMPRESS. People like to let formal lingo creep into their writing, as if that formality gives them more authority. Your signature should express your authority, not your words. Instead of saying "aforesaid" and "heretofore," "herewith is" and "notwithstanding," why don't you just go to the more casual way of writing "that," "until now," "here is," and "in spite of"? "The aforesaid information, herewith defines your legal rights," can be "That information tells you what legal rights you have."

Instead of saying "the undersigned," you can certainly refer to yourself as "I." The best writers impress their readers through language that doesn't call attention to itself. You don't want your readers to be distracted by the language itself; you want them to be moved by the content. It's like wearing a very fancy or distracting outfit; it calls attention to you but away from the subject that you're trying to present. There's nothing wrong with plain talk to get your point across.

Here are some final thoughts on relaxing stuffy language: keep your writing as direct, concise, and precise as you can.

Don't use a general word if the context calls for a specific one. Be as definite as you can. The best writers know that the more specific are the image and the idea that they create in their writing, the more specific is the image that their readers visualize. For example, instead of "aircraft," say "plane." Instead of saying "plane," say "DC-10." Instead of saying "improved costs," say "lowered costs." Instead of saying "I'll call you soon," say "I'll call you next Tuesday."

Tell them in which direction you're going. "We have improved our product." Is it faster, cheaper? What specifically is the improvement you're talking about? "Communication," someone once said, "is never having to say, 'huh?' after you've read a memo." Bringing your reader next to you saves time and money, creating a positive, warm, and welcome image that no amount of advertising or budgeting can bring to you. The more specific and concrete you are, the more you come across as an authoritative, responsible writer.

Your writing is the consistent, most powerful way to create a positive image for yourself and your company. It's the least expensive, yet most effective way that you can project life and efficiency to all the people you need to communicate with regularly. SPEAKWRITE "RULE 3: Avoid Stuffy Language," is the cornerstone for all your business memo skills.

AVOID STUFFY LANGUAGE

Stuffy: *We are in receipt of your recent letter concerning your account.*

Relaxed: **We received your recent letter about your accounts**

Stuffy: *We are endeavoring to minimize problems where feasible.*

Relaxed: **We're trying to reduce problems, where possible.**

Stuffy: *It is realized that you will have to effect numerous modifications.*

Relaxed: **We realize you'll have to make many changes.**

VERBS

- ☐ USE ACTION VERBS, NOT "TO BE" VERBS
- ☐ USE THE ACTIVE, NOT THE PASSIVE VOICE

RULE 4: USE STRONG VERBS

Some people enter my writing seminars with painful memories of their junior high school grammar classes. My only grammar lesson in the SPEAKWRITE System concerns learning the value of the verb. Verbs create power in your writing. The central word in your sentence is the verb. It's the action word, the only one that can actually do something for you. Most people rely on weak or inactive verbs rather than strong and active verbs to move their sentences along. Their sentences sit rather than move on the page. That's exactly the opposite of what you want to accomplish.

The two kinds of verbs are action and being. For starters, try to eliminate "is," "are," "was," "will be," "can," or "should." Avoid overusing all forms of the verb "to be."

Avoid Overusing

AVOID THESE WORDS:

am	had
are	has
be	have
became	is
become	should
been	was
being	will
can	will be
could	would

Use action verbs instead!

compose	negotiate
coordinate	reorganize
delegate	participate
demonstrate	present
establish	propose
evaluate	revise
generate	schedule
invent	streamline
motivate	supervise

Use action verbs which move your sentence along; they communicate movement, power, and direction. Whenever you can, turn a being verb into an action verb, and you will enhance your sentence tremendously.

Here's an example.

```
He is a strong writer.
```

The verb you want is already there, masked as another part of speech. I call this finding the "smothered verb." Where is it? In the noun, in this sentence. Look for the strongest word, which is "writer." Turn that into your verb, and you've got a very powerful and effective sentence:

```
He writes strongly.
```

or

```
He writes effectively.
```

The improvement is 100 percent. Here is another example:

```
My new assistant is negligent in her work.
```

Look at the verb "is." It does nothing to enhance the sentence. The key to the statement is the word "negligent," or maybe "work." If you scan that sentence with the verbal Geiger counter, you pick up both of those words. Rewrite the sentence:

```
My new assistant neglects some of her work.
```

(a definite improvement), or

```
My new assistant works in a negligent manner.
```

or

```
My new assistant works irresponsibly (or
irregularly, inconsistently...).
```

Some other frequently used verbs are weak rather than strong. But it's not possible to avoid them all the time. Avoid using "to do," "to make," "to seem," "to appear," "to be," and "to get." Although all are grammatically correct, they lack power.

Let your verbs work more. Look at this sentence:

```
This directive is applicable to all personnel who
make use of our system.
```

Our weak verbs show up again: "is" and "make." Without having to search at all for new words, you can tighten up this sentence by writing, "This directive applies to all personnel who use our system." These simple changes create meaning, power, and impact in the entire sentence.

Certain nouns frequently smother active verbs. "Authorization" is one of them. It's also a popular word in the business world:

```
The authorization for the trip was given by my
supervisor.
```

How about writing,

```
My supervisor authorized the trip.
```

You may notice that words ending in "ion," such as "authorization," "production," "hesitation," "completion," often smother verbs. These shifts aren't difficult, and they create more powerful business writing.

The second way to strengthen the verb in your sentences is to move from the passive to the active voice. This is a subtle shift. Here's how it works: when trying to understand the difference between passive and active voice, think in terms of the types of people you know. A passive person lets things happen to him or her. An active person makes things happen. The same is true in business memo sentences. Passive voice verbs delay the action; they let something happen to the actor rather than having the actor go out and accomplish. They pose word order problems:

```
The plant was inspected by the supervisor.
```

Who's supposed to be the actor in that sentence? The supervisor, yet that person is receiving the action. All you have to do to move your sentence from passive to active is ask yourself, "Who is doing what to whom?" In that sentence the supervisor is performing the action to the plant, so switch the word order around:

```
The supervisor inspected the plant.
```

That switch does three very important things. First, it shifts the sentence from passive to active; now the doer performs rather than receives the action. Second, the switch eliminates the weak "being" verb and substitutes an active, strong verb, "inspected." And third, it tightens and shortens your sentence.

You win all the way around when you move from the passive to the active voice in your business memos. A verb in the passive voice combines any form of the verb "to be" with the past participle of the main verb; that is, the passive uses "am," "is," "are," "was," "were," "be," "being," "been" plus a main verb that usually ends in "en" or "ed." In this sentence, who are the actors?

```
Appropriate clothing will be worn by all personnel.
```

Just place the actors at the beginning of the sentence, and it will now read,

```
All personnel will wear appropriate clothing.
```

Or, do this if you want to give a directive:

```
Wear appropriate clothing. (Or, you can always
soften your directive with "please....")
```

It's tighter, cleaner, and certainly more direct and effective. Another example:

```
He was regarded poorly by his supervisors.
```

That is a passive voice sentence.

```
His supervisors regarded him poorly.
```

That example brings up an interesting point. Often people hide behind the passive and duck responsibility for something that they feel, decide, or do. Many performance evaluations employ passive voice verbs, especially when there is bad news.

```
A poor job was done by Nancy Anne.
```

Another way to know if you're writing in the passive voice is if you use the word "by" and follow it by what should be the subject of your sentence. Here's an example:

```
The card was issued by The ABC Club.
```

Instead write:

```
The ABC Club issued the card.
```

In a passive voice sentence the verb always precedes "by." That's another way to spot them.

Are you thinking it might be difficult to let go of lengthy phrases, passive verbs, and long words because you won't sound intelligent? If that's your initial reaction to SPEAKWRITE, you're not alone.

But our nation is changing its habits. A large southwestern bank gives its top executives only half sheets of paper to write on. The bank knows that when given a full sheet, most of us will fill it up. Management shouldn't spend too much time on their writing, and the half sheets limit the inbred training from school for length and wordiness.

A successful midwestern company has a very interesting corporate policy. If an employee sends to management a letter or memo that is longer than one page, the offended reader stamps it "unread" and returns it to the writer.

Why not bring some of these changes into your own company?

The Perfect MEMO!

6

REFINE IT

I remember a woman who attended a writing class for hospital employees. When asked what she wanted to learn at the session, she replied, "To be able to turn out perfect copy the first time." Immediately I smiled. She knew why. There is no way that any good writer can turn out perfect copy consistently the first time.

By chance we can occasionally do that. But real writers know that good writing means rewriting. By mastering the steps in this book, you will turn out better copy the first time. Still, this final step, "Refine It," teaches you how to transform your memo from ordinary to outstanding. In this section, you will learn about tools to polish, refine, and perfect your memo to make it memorable for your reader.

REACHING THE FINAL MINUTES

Your memo sits in front of you. It must go out shortly. You probably want to proofread and send it right now. Don't! Put it away for as long as you can before you give it the final reread.

It's very hard to be an objective critic of your own writing. I hope you like yourself enough to have an ego that doesn't want to criticize or be too hard on what you've written. Most people look at what they've just written and say, "That's pretty good." And so they send out copy with errors that might not be obvious to them, but will be apparent to someone else. Or, they look and say "This is awful!" and tear it up! So, after you've written your memo, put it away from one to twenty-four hours. Then come back to it fresh. Pretend that someone else has written your memo. Then critique it with an objective eye. Read your memo with these questions in mind:

☐ Have I written to the audience that I want to address?

☐ Have I used the appropriate tone for whoever is going to get it?

If it's an informal, casual memo:

☐ Is my language casual, relaxed?

If it's a more formal or distant audience:

☐ Have I established a more conservative or formal tone?

Those are questions you kept in mind when you wrote your orginal draft. For your final proofreading you want to make sure that you have absolutely adhered to the guidelines you established when you first began to write.

Check your purpose:

- ☐ Have I accomplished my original purpose in writing this memo?

- ☐ Did I ask for what I want?

With those guidelines in mind, you can become an objective critic of your memo. Now, go through your writing quickly. See how the entire memo reads. Try reading it out loud. After all, if you're using the SPEAKWRITE it sounds is how it's going to read. Your primary focus is still:

- ☐ How would I speak this?

- ☐ Is my language natural and comfortable?

That practice will help you pick up language that doesn't work, pompous words, and phrases that are literary rather than conversational. Your reading the memo aloud will tell you how it will sound to your reader.

THE PROOF IS IN YOUR READING

Here are several other proofreading techniques.

If you want to get true distance from something you've written, run your memo through a copy machine. Then critique it as though someone else had written it. Most people are better editors than they are writers. This technique lets you play editor.

PROOFREADING TECHNIQUES

- ☐ LET IT SIT
- ☐ READ IT ALOUD
- ☐ EXCHANGE IT WITH A COLLEAGUE
- ☐ READ IT BACKWARDS
- ☐ CHECK REFERENCE MATERIALS
- ☐ MAKE IT PERFECT!

Try rereading your memo in a different light or a different room from the one in which you wrote it. This gives you additional distance and objectivity.

Read your memo into a tape recorder. As you listen to the memo, you will hear it with added objectivity. "No," you might say, "that phrase is awkward," or, "I've got too many words in that sentence," or "That sentence just doesn't sound right." Again, hearing the memo gives you a better, clearer idea of exactly how it will sound to your prospective reader. A recent convenience-store client with a long-standing spelling problem told me that reading his memo aloud let him catch spelling mistakes he would have overlooked.

Read your memo backwards! That might sound like a gimmick, but if you read it backwards and follow your eye across the page from right to left, you will be thrown out of your normal way of relating to your words and phrases. You'll notice spelling errors, repeated words, and punctuation mistakes that you wouldn't find in a routine rereading. Many people are so accustomed to or bored with reading what they just wrote that their eyes automatically skip over glaring typographical errors. However, if you're reading the page backwards, you will see problems you might not otherwise spot.

One of the most challenging learning and critiquing methods is to find colleagues in your office to read your memos. You can do the same for them. In that way you give each other ideas and feedback on your writing. It's another way of deepening relationships in your company and finding out that other people struggle with the same writing problems that you do.

At first people are hesitant to take this step because of privacy, modesty, or reluctance to share their writing difficulties with others. But after they've done it once or twice, they find it a profitable and enjoyable experience. Also, they get clear feedback on their writing—the kind that they always wanted in school but never received. Instead of receiving a paper blighted with red marks, they hear constructive criticism and helpful ideas. A second party can pick up errors in organization, proofreading, and grammar that you might not spot yourself.

Those are some technical ways of reviewing your memo to ensure that what you have in the final draft is a far stronger product. You can make up your own set of guidelines for a final inspection. I'll give you a few guidelines, and you can add to them your own specifications and needs. It's like assembling a car. Before the car leaves the assembly line, the inspectors look it over with quality assurance guidelines in mind. They don't let that car leave the plant until it has passed maximum safety and product specifications. Well, neither should you let your memo!

When I worked with the convenience-store manager with the spelling problem, we devised the following final evaluation checklist:

EVALUATION

On a scale of 1 to 5, please rate this piece of writing. (1 = poor, 5 = outstanding)

The writer:	1	2	3	4	5
Decreases sentence length					
Omits needless words					
Avoids stuffy language					
Uses strong verbs					
Punctuates correctly					
Organizes effectively					
Uses supporting material					

He began to use it for everything he wrote, and so can you!

MAKING THE FINAL INSPECTION

Read through your writing quickly. Make sure it reads smoothly. Do it in conjunction with Westroots Rules of Writing. Ask yourself, do I:

- ☐ Decrease my sentence length?

- ☐ Omit needless words?

- ☐ Avoid stuffy language?

- ☐ Use strong verbs?

These are the four major guidelines for reading through your writing. They make your writing specific, technically accurate, and stylistically correct.

THE KEY TO ORGANIZATION

Now look at your organization. Do this quickly and easily. Determine at once whether you have organized your memo in the most effective and powerful manner. Simply circle the main point of your memo and make sure it comes early.

Read the memo that follows and circle the main point. The writer starts with reasons, justifications, and preliminary information, and then puts the main point much too late in the memo. The reader has to search too long and too far before reaching the main point. This organization works for a mystery story—Agatha Christie would welcome this organization—but you can't afford it.

```
DATE:      October 29, 19XX
TO:        Dan Manley
FROM:      Ray King
RE:        EXTENDED DAY AND BUS TIMING


Dan, I am sure you have heard this all
before many times, however, I feel you need
to know that some of our students' parents
are becoming concerned about the extended
day.

Before Master Plan, our hours were 9:00 a.m.
to 3:00 p.m. Since that time, the bus office
has dictated our time. As you know, our
official time, as set by that office this
year, is 9:20 a.m. to 3:40 p.m. The real
world for us though is 9:00 a.m.-9:30 a.m.,
depending on the bus, to 3:10 p.m.-4:20 p.m.

The feeling is that the longer day tires the
children so much more that many are becoming
ill. In addition, the Children's
Convalescent Center director, Ellen Watts,
tells us the bus timing in the afternoon
causes daily problems and frustration for
them.
```

**main
idea
→**

```
We need some assistance in trying to
renegotiate school hours and afternoon bus
schedules. Is it possible to get a waiver
for this particular school because of the
nature of handicaps here?
```

Strong corporate writing starts with the main point first. So, if you circle the main point in this memo, which we have indicated with an arrow, you will quickly see that the writer delays the main point until the end. Read through your own writing. If your main point is at the end, circle it and move it up earlier. Your eye and your ear will quickly point out what's important.

Now let's talk about some specific words, phrases, and ideas you want to leave out. We talked earlier about the phrases "it is" and "there are." Flag and delete them. Writers often lean on these phrases to begin their sentences, but these phrases are empty, add nothing, and sap the vitality of much corporate writing.

Avoid using an excessive number of abbreviations and explanations. You're writing a memo, not a lengthy proposal or a documented report or a dictionary of terminology. Let the readers ask you if they have further questions, or want more text. However, in all my years of writing shorter memos, I've never had anyone call me and ask, "Could you please write more next time?"

TRANSITIONS: HOW YOU MOVE. As you read from paragraph to paragraph, make sure that your organization is clear and that there is a smooth flow of ideas throughout. You can accomplish this flow by using effective openings, clear topic sentences, and smooth transitions. The Appendix includes a list of useful transitions. These are words like "however," "moreover," "nevertheless," and "therefore," or some of the more relaxed transitions like "but," "and," "so," and "first." Regardless of the set of transitions you choose, I recommend that you have a modest, yet definite, sprinkling of transitions from paragraph to paragraph, idea to idea. This practice helps your reader move easily and smoothly from one idea to the next. After all, you want to be understood. Like using any tool, however, you don't want to overdo it; one transition per paragraph is usually enough.

Another way to move smoothly between paragraphs is to take a word from the last sentence of one paragraph and use it in the first sentence of the next paragraph. Here's an example:

```
You should attract many viewers with these excellent
locations.

Many people have reserved these locations to
exhibit...
```

In addition, try using a single sentence to make a transition between paragraphs. For example:

```
Reports show that people take road trips based on
the price of gasoline. Some organizations, like
hotels, want to keep the price of gas down to
increase traveling—and business.

But authorities prove that the price of gas doesn't
necessarily reflect the amount of road trips people
take.

They showed that although the price of gas went down
in some cases, hotel reservations stayed the same or
even decreased. Apparently, other factors influence
road trips—the cost of foreign travel, weather
conditions, and the prices of other necessities such
as clothing and food.
```

Another way to make a transition is to use headers to announce the contents of the following paragraph. Here's an example:

```
                    PAY DAY
Pay day will be on Monday. The 15th falls on the
weekend this month.
```

VISUALS: THE OVERALL LOOK. Next, look for visual guideposts. Have you divided your memo so that it reads effectively? Have you organized and segmented your writing in a clear way? Have you used subject lines? Have you indicated at the top of the memo to whom it goes and why it's being sent? Have you used subparagraphs? If it is a lengthy memo, have you divided it into subsections that will work effectively for your reader?

We talked earlier about white space. Look at your memo. Is it visually pleasing? Or is it a solid block of type? Are you drawn into your memo, or are you pushed away from it? If you feel pushed away, so will your reader. To prevent this reaction, break up your paragraphs, making them shorter and even more effective. Create some lists or white space to rest your reader's eyes and give them some visual variety.

Create visuals:

☐ Paragraphs

☐ Lists

☐ Subject lines

☐ Headers

PRESENTING YOUR KEY IDEAS. Finally, have you highlighted key ideas and indicated their relationships? You can do this using lists, subheads, parallel phrasing, and underlined ideas; As you read through your memo, try to imagine that you are the reader, not the writer. After all, you're trying to reach your readers, not yourself. How will they respond? What will they think of your writing? Will they be moved to action? Will they understand exactly what you're talking about? That, of course, is your aim.

Write your memo and imagine your name is on the "To," not the "From," line. How does the memo read now? Is it persuasive and clear, or is it offensive and confusing? These vital questions will give you the essential feedback.

Test market your memo before you send it out. Either test it on somebody else in your company, or imagine that you are the test market yourself. Does it read well? Does it look attractive? Will it move your reader to take action or gather information? If all these requirements have been satisfied, then you have written a memo that speaks well for you.

This memo was written by a hospital administrator. Would you have sent it? What recommendations would you make? Look at it with your own guidelines in mind. Read the memo carefully:

```
To:        Sam Green, Vice President, Administration
From:      Joan Williams, Assistant Administrator
Subject:   QUALITY ASSURANCE COMMITTEE MEETING
           JANUARY 11, 19XX
```

I attended the first meeting of the 19XX Quality Assurance Committee today! A statement was made by Dr. Brown that for the last two years he served as Peer Review Committee Chairman and prior to that on the Audit Committee for Internal Medicine and they never had any direction or idea of what needed to be done. This came up because Dr. Adams states to all of the committee members that QA items must be on all agendas.

My concern is that Dr. Hunson is responsible for QA and Audit and Peer Review Committee meetings and should be attending these meetings and **providing that direction.** I believe it is written into his job description. Perhaps he has been sending only the QA Coordinator to the meetings and she really only pulls charts and does minutes and helps with the coordination of the activities. Dr. Hunson must provide the direction, and especially this year when we have more new Chairmen. I would like to suggest that Dr. Hunson's job description be reviewed and revised and I would like to suggest that this subject be discussed with Dr. Smith, Chairman of Quality Assurance. I would also like to suggest that Dr. Hunson be asked to attend every Department Specialty Meeting and discuss what types of Quality Assurance items should be addressed, how the topics should be picked, and how his Department will assist the committees/departments in carrying out these assigned responsibilities.

I sincerely appreciate your consideration of my request. I see this as a major issue that should be taken care of immediately. I would like to see the new Committees provided with **direction and appropriate** assistance from Dr. Hunson.

```
jw
```

P.S. Dr. Brown also stated that all the time he
served on the Audit and Peer Review Committees he
was not aware that there was a Quality Assurance
Committee and he felt that perhaps the committee
should provide more direction to the Audit and Peer
Review Committees. I feel this is an excellent
suggestion and since Hank serves on the QA Committee
he should be the liaison between QA Committee and
the other Committees.

All right, now that you've read this memo, look at a suggested
revision:

To: Sam Green,
         Vice-President/Administration
From: Joan Williams,
         Assistant Administrator
Subject: Responsibility of Quality Assurance
         Committee
Date: February 1, 19XX

I have several recommendations as a result of my
attendance at the first Quality Assurance Committee
meeting of 19XX:

❑ I recommend that Dr. Hunson, whose
   responsibilities include the QA, Peer Review,
   and Audit Committees, should attend all their
   meetings, providing direction and assistance.

❑ I also recommend that Dr. Hunson be asked to
   attend all department specialty meetings to
   discuss what types of QA items should be
   addressed, how the topics should be chosen, and
   how his department can help the committees/
   departments carry out their QA assignments.

❑ Finally, I feel that Dr. Hunson's job
   description should be reviewed and revised to
   clarify any confusion that may exist concerning
   his exact responsibilities in connection with
   these important committees.

I consider QA a major issue that should be taken
care of immediately. I sincerely appreciate your
attention to my recommendations.

The second memo is easier to read; it is more appealing to the eye; it has better organization; and it yells out, "Read me, read me!"

You realize that these memos are longer than usual. Also notice that your attention wandered, you wanted to skip on to new material, and you didn't really pay attention to the text. Well, the same goes for your memos. There's no absolute rule about maximum length of a memo. However, memos that are longer than one page get skimmed rather than read.

A well-known Baltimore accountant once admitted that he gives himself thirty seconds to read a memo regardless of the length. If it's two pages, he gives it just thirty seconds; if it's one-half page, again thirty seconds. Needless to say, the shorter one gets read much more thoroughly.

So keep that limit in mind when you write your memos. Pace them like the best thirty-second commercial you've ever watched.

FINAL RETOUCHES. Any rough draft you refine once or twice improves each time. So if you have done all the preliminary work, why not spend some time on refining? The refinement process is like getting dressed and putting the finishing touches on yourself. You wouldn't go to an interview wearing a well-pressed suit that looks fine yet wearing a tie that has a big stain.

Many people commit this type of error in writing. They spend a lot of time on the initial draft; they get it looking fine; they type it on the best stationery; and they use a format worthy of attention. Yet in the final stages, there is a spelling error, a misplaced comma, or a grammatical mistake that undermines the authority, authenticity, and clarity of their memo.

A client told me recently of receiving an important letter spotted with the writer's coffee and lunch! The topic was appetizing; the messy look was not! Also look out for lipstick smudges, erasures, and other signs of hasty "final touches."

PUNCTUATION POLISH

POLISHING PUNCTUATION. An interesting incident happened in one of my early SPEAKWRITE seminars. We were discussing when and how to use punctuation—and also the fact that business writing today demands fewer rather than more marks of punctuation. An alert woman raised her hand. In front of the group she confessed, "I like to use a lot of different marks of punctuation, just so my readers will think I'm more intelligent." She continued, "I'm not even certain that the marks I use are correct, but I figure that the more semicolons, question marks, colons, and exclamation marks people find in my writing, the more intelligent they'll believe I am." It's so typical of what people tend to do with all aspects of their writing!

The sad thing is, though, that your audiences won't see you as smarter. They'll perceive you as wordy, obscure, pretentious.

Punctuation is a vital part and necessary factor in good writing. In fact, the best writers know that they can have wonderful ideas and cleverly phrased sentences. But poor and inaccurate punctuation still ruins their writing.

THE POWER OF PROPER PUNCTUATION. The use of punctuation demands a book in itself. When I am employed by companies, I present a separate eight-hour session on punctuation. That barely covers commas! I strongly recommend that in conjunction with a good grammar and reference text, you purchase a punctuation manual. Several such manuals are listed in the bibliography in the Appendix. I will highlight here some factors about punctuation that good business writers need to know.

PUT IN THE PERIOD. The mark of punctuation most needed in business writing is the period. Why? Because most writers create sentences that are much too long. They don't insert the period soon enough. When do you put in the period? As we said earlier, after 17 words or less. This mark of punctuation gives your reader a chance to pause, to digest what you've just written, and then to move smoothly to your next thought.

Instead of writing:

```
Your analysis of the brochure we published
yesterday was coherent but I still would like some
more concise explanations because many of your
examples were vague.
```

Write:

```
Your analysis of the brochure we published yesterday
was coherent. But I still would like some more
concise explanations. Many of your examples were
vague.
```

CURBING COMMA FEVER. The next vital mark of punctuation is the comma. English has dozens of rules for using the comma, and your grammar reference book will show them to you. Look at the sentence below and see how the writer has linked two independent or complete thoughts with a comma.

> You should have received your check, we mailed it to you on February 20.

That's what editors call a "comma splice," or a run-on sentence. You should separate these two sentences with a period, not a comma. Keep this rule in mind: commas can't separate sentences! Some of the other situations for using commas are between items in a series, between lengthy introductory phrases and clauses, and between two clauses separated by conjunctions. But you will come across these needs and uses as you're writing. Just keep in mind that the comma is a powerful and effective mark of punctuation for separating thoughts and phrases in your memo writing.

A lot of people have "comma fever"; that is, when they don't know what else to do with their punctuation, they insert a comma just to show any kind of pause or break. Although the comma is a necessary mark of punctuation, using it can be overdone. You don't want to break up the flow of a sentence unnecessarily. In fact, keep in mind a SPEAKWRITE rule: if you don't have a reason to use a comma, leave it out. The comma should not come too often in the flow of a sentence; otherwise, what you have is a choppy list, rather than smoothly connected words. Readers are more offended by excess punctuation than by not enough.

> Avoid sentences like these:
>
> Please, analyze, prepare, and evaluate, then, print
> out a new, complete brochure, so that James, the
> editor, can reread your work.
>
> That idea, which contradicts everyone else's, may be
> good, but it's a problem raiser, and we should, if
> we can, avoid problems, at all costs.

Delete commas and any other excesses. If you need to, begin new sentences where commas exist. For example:

> Please analyze, prepare, and evaluate the text. Then
> print out a new complete brochure so that James, our
> editor, can reread your work.
>
> That idea contradicts everyone else's. It may be
> good, but it is a issue raiser. We should, if we
> can, avoid problems.

SECRETS FOR THE SEMICOLON. Now what about the semicolon? A lot of people get confused about the semicolon, not really understanding its uses. Look at the sentence below and see how the writer has used the semicolon:

> The original materials came from our Charleston
> plant; the finished product was made in Toledo.

That's one long sentence that could have been divided in two or separated by a comma and a conjunction. But the two parts of the sentence are very closely connected, and the semicolon shows the close line between them. Also note that after the semicolon, you do not use a capital letter. The unit is technically one complete thought. An alternative revision reads as follows:

```
The original materials came from our Charleston
plant, but the finished product was made in Toledo.
```

Both examples are grammatically correct. It is up to you to choose the style you want. By being able to use both styles, you can add variety to your memos.

KNOWING ABOUT COLONS. First cousin to the semi-colon is the colon. The most effective use of the colon in business writing is to introduce a list. The colon means "the following" and should never be used following a verb or preposition. So when you write a sentence with a list or items to follow, the colon works this way:

```
To:        Guest Service Agents
From:      Front Office Manager
Date:      December 24,19XX
Subject:   CONCIERGE CASH TICKETS

These are the procedures for posting concierge cash
tickets:

  ❏ Post the concierge tour amount to the guest
    folio.

  ❏ Post the cash amount to the guest folio.

  ❏ Place the cash credit slip with your deposit
    envelope.

  ❏ Place the concierge slips with your work to go
    to the night audit.

  ❏ Do not handle cash; the concierge will deposit
    it.
```

PUTTING IN THE APOSTROPHE. The apostrophe is a mark of punctuation that many people don't know how to pronounce, much less use. The two major uses of it are to show possession and contraction. First, possessives show ownership. "The manager's staff" shows that the staff belongs to the manager. That's not much of a problem. Most people get in trouble trying to decide where to put the apostrophe when the word ends in "s" or when a word is plural. Look at the following examples to see the correct uses of the apostrophe in possessives.

Singular	Singular Possessive	Plural	Plural Possessive
employer	employer's offices	employers	employers' offices
week	week's work	weeks	two weeks' work
dollar	dollar's worth	dollars	5 dollars' worth
woman	woman's purse	women	women's purses
Athens	Athen's ruins		

A strong set of rules for deciding where to put the apostrophe is:

☐ Decide if the word showing possession is singular or plural.

☐ If it is singular, add 's.

☐ If it is plural, and doesn't end in s, add 's.

☐ If it is plural, and ends in s, add 'to the *right* of the s.'

CAPTURING CONTRACTIONS. Second, use apostrophes in contractions. But, should you use contractions at all in business writing? Ten years ago most business memos, letters, and reports avoided them. Words like "cannot, do not, should not" appeared instead of "can't, don't," and "shouldn't." However, with the trend toward more relaxed writing, there is nothing wrong with using "can't, don't," and "shouldn't" if these words maintain rather than undermine the tone and purpose of your memo.

However, if you are using contractions in one part of your memo, use them throughout. Look at the following sentence that was written by a well-intended business writer. Notice that what you see is a mixed rather than consistent use of contracted and noncontracted forms.

> You **didn't** get your check because you **did not** send us the correct form. It **doesn't** matter when you return the form. **You are** entitled to your benefits.

If you mix together contractions and noncontracted forms, you're shifting back and forth between the formal and the informal tone. That can create confusion and an inconsistent tone in your memo. Again, there is nothing wrong with using contractions if in fact your tone is informal, especially for in-house memos.

Imagine that your boss wrote you this memo:

> We can't meet tomorrow afternoon at 5 p.m. So we'll reschedule the meeting next Monday at lunch. I hope it's convenient for you.

The same memo could have been written this way:

> "We cannot meet tomorrow at 5 p.m. So we will reschedule the meeting for next Monday at noon. I hope it is convenient for you."

The content is the same, but the tone is not. The second tone is more formal and distancing, and perhaps does not seem as pleasant to the reader. After all, imagine that you are the listener. You want to be communicated with like a comrade. Contractions can sometimes relax your words enough so that even bad news can be softened.

Here's a partial list of common contractions and their noncontracted forms.

aren't	are not	isn't	is not
can't	cannot	it's	it is
couldn't	could not	she'll	she will
didn't	did not	shouldn't	should not
doesn't	does not	there's	there is
don't	do not	they're	they are
hadn't	had not	we'll	we will
hasn't	has not	who's	who is
haven't	have not	won't	will not
he'll	he will	wouldn't	would not
I'll	I will	you'll	you will

PUTTING IN PARENTHESES. What about parentheses? Many people use parentheses when they don't know exactly where to place an idea. They reason, "Well, if my reader doesn't want to read this, he doesn't have to, but I'll put it in parentheses just to cover myself." That procedure doesn't work well, especially in business writing. Why not? It breaks up the flow of an otherwise smoothly written memo; it distracts the reader from your main point or idea. Look at the following memo and see how the writer places a major body of information in parentheses.

```
Most sophisticated PC users recognize the offline
systems are only marginally appropriate for
personal computers (see attached copy of article
from PC Week, April 3, 19XX, Page 6, for a
discussion of the inappropriateness of Yest standby
systems for use with an IBM PC. Yest is the largest
manufacturer of standby systems.), and in no case
adequate if a modem is in use.
```

Most readers' response to this memo is either confusion or annoyance. In fact when I use this example in my punctuation seminar, most participants skip over it. People don't want to struggle through copy in order to understand it. If you use parentheses for material that you are not sure belongs in your memo, omit the material because it is of little importance. Or, if it is important, do not put it in parentheses. Putting it in parentheses relegates it to a status of lesser importance, and the reader will ignore its importance. When you have to put information in parentheses, the best way is by placing your entire sentence in parentheses. The worst way is by beginning a sentence, putting a parenthetical unit in the middle, and then completing your sentence.

That method doesn't work well stylistically or organization-ally. Look at the preceding memo and see how the writer broke up an important sentence with parentheses and destroyed the flow of the sentence. Improve the sentence by rewriting it this way:

```
Most sophisticated PC users recognize that off-line
systems are only marginally appropriate for
personal computers and in no case adequate if a
modem is in use. (See attached copy of article from
PC Week, April 2,1986, page 6, for a discussion of
the inappropriateness of Yest standby systems for
use with an IBM PC. Yest is the largest
manufacturer of standby systems.)
```

Parentheses are also necessary when you use the lengthy name of a company or document and then present the abbreviated form or acronym of the name. The parentheses should enclose the abbreviated or acronym form so that you can continue to use that form throughout the rest of the memo. This is an acceptable and necessary way of presenting an abbreviation or acronym. However, don't use abbreviations in your memo unless you are certain your reader knows what they stand for.

QUOTING QUOTATION MARKS. Quotation marks are necessary and functional marks of punctuation. Most people know that quotation marks are used to indicate what someone has said. The problem is not when but how to use them. Here are the basic uses for quotation marks:

Rule 1: Periods and commas are always placed within quotation marks. Example: He said, "Let's go soon."

Rule 2: Semicolons and colons are always placed outside quotation marks.

Example: He said, "Let's go soon"; we didn't go.

Rule 3: Exclamation points and question marks are placed either within or outside the quotation marks, depending on the sense of the sentence.

Example: Have you read "Business News"?

We are going to discuss the question "What is our strategy on the Miller Project?"

He shouted, "Watch out!"

Watch out for "bozos"!

Again, a complete grammar book will provide sound guidelines for using quotation marks, but these three rules should help. Punctuation need not be a terribly complex subject, and you certainly don't have to go back to seventh-grade English in order to learn it. However, using correct punctuation will increase your confidence.

? AND ! The last two marks of punctuation which often signal the end of sentences are the question mark and the exclamation point. Many business writers are hesitant to use them. I recommend that if you are trying to achieve variety in vocabulary, style, and format, you should do some experimenting, using both interrogative and exclamatory sentences.

What's wrong with starting a memo with a question? That's a very effective way of drawing your readers into your memo and getting them involved in the subject matter. Have you ever heard a speech in which the speaker opens up with a question? Immediately, the audience looks up. They are involved. They're drawn into the subject. You can do the same by opening a memo or a letter with a question, showing your readers that you are speaking to them, engaging their attention rather than speaking at them or to them. "What are your thoughts on the Simington project?" "Can you arrange a meeting in my office at 5 p.m. tomorrow afternoon?" Those are effective memo openers that show originality and variety, and draw your reader into your topic.

To show emotion, there's nothing wrong with writing, "That was a great report that you sent me on the Nielson meeting yesterday afternoon!"

Unconventional punctuation, like offbeat vocabulary, can be overdone and overused. But a modest sprinkling of out-of-the ordinary punctuation marks energizes your writing and sets you off as someone with style and flair.

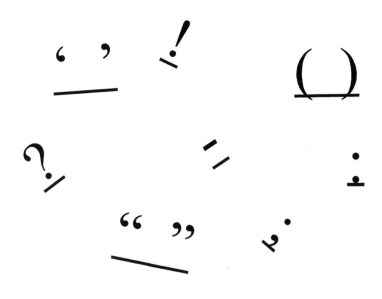

FINALE

With these basic guidelines on punctuation, grammar, structure, and format, you can judge if your memo is polished and refined. By now, you have the SPEAKWRITE skills for writing a memo. You have the advantage of your outstanding memo; you have written something compact, concise, casual, and correct.

People will look forward to reading what you have written. They will welcome a memo from your office and will act on it promptly. The memo will reflect the work you've done on it. You can take these skills into any kind of writing, from a memo to a lengthy proposal, and know that you are writing with authority, creativity, and correctness.

A well-known writer once said that people remember most material they read first and last. What comes in between is important, but it doesn't stick with readers the way beginnings and endings do.

Why is this message important right now? Well, you've read *The Perfect Memo,* and you're ready to write. What's the most important message to give you right now? It's that you *can do it.* You can write with confidence, competence, and excitement, knowing that you're reaching your audience with contemporary, conversational, and concise language. They'll praise you for your craft, and hopefully, send you a perfect memo in return. What could be a greater reward than that?

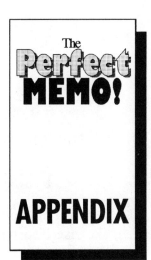

APPENDIX

TRANSITIONS/CONNECTIVES

Link sentences by using such transitional expressions as:

ADDITION: moreover, further, furthermore, besides, and, and then, likewise, also, nor, too, again, in addition, equally important, next, first, second, third, etc., finally, last, lastly

CONTRAST: but, yet, and yet, however, still, nevertheless, on the other hand, on the contrary, after all, notwithstanding, for all that, in contrast to this, at the same time, although this may be true, otherwise

COMPARISON: similarly, likewise, in like manner

PURPOSE: to this end, for this purpose, with this object

RESULT: hence, therefore, accordingly, consequently, thus, thereupon, wherefore, as a result

TIME: meanwhile, at length, immediately, soon, after a few days, in the meantime, afterward, later, now

PLACE: here, beyond, nearby, opposite to, adjacent to, on the opposite side

SUMMARY, REPETITION, EXEMPLIFICATION, INTENSIFICATION: to sum up, in brief, on the whole, in sum, in short, as I have said, in other words, to be sure, as has been noted, for example, for instance, in fact, indeed, in any event

Use short spoken transitions instead of long, bookish ones. Save long transitions for variety. By using short ones, you help set an ordinary tone for the rest of what you say.

More normal	*More Relaxed*
consequently	so
however	but
in addition	also
nevertheless	still

REDUNDANT REDUNDANCIES

at this point in time	plan in advance	resume again
one a.m. in the morning	part and parcel	only unique
	two equal halveS	right and proper
original founder	black in color	basic essentials
round in shape	final conclusion	continue on
consensus of opinion	refer back to	end result
	reason why	necessary requisite
close proximity	mutual cooperation	
may possibly		
safe and sound		

POMPOUS WORDS AND WINDY PHRASES

Instead of:	*Use:*
call your attention to the fact that	remind you
an example of this is the fact that	for example
afford an opportunity	allow
due to the fact that	because
exhibit a tendency to	tend to
for the purpose of	for, to
in reference to	about, regarding
in view of the fact that	because
in the normal course of our procedure	normally
it is interesting to note that	(delete this phrase)
in the majority of circumstances	usually

LITTLE QUALIFIERS

a number of	a great many	more or less
considerably	as far as we know	essentially
generally	nearly	little
on the whole	reasonably	quite
to some degree	possibly	pretty
just	seems	very

JARGON . . .

. . . conceals a simple idea in a thick fog of words, using circumlocutions instead of going straight to the point, preferring abstract nouns to concrete ones, concentrating on sound rather than sense.

proactive	quantify	overview
paradigm	parameter	conceptualize
prioritize	facilitate	impact (verb)

SIMPLER WORDS AND PHRASES

Instead of	*Try*
accompany	go with
accomplish	carry out, do
accorded	given
accordingly	so
accrue	add, gain
accurate	correct, exact, right
additional	added, more, other
address	discuss
addressees	you
addressees are requested	(omit), please
adjacent to	next to
advantageous	helpful
adversely impact on	hurt, set back
advise	recommend, tell
afford an opportunity	allow, let
aircraft	plane
allocate	divide, give
anticipate	expect
a number of	some

Instead of	Try
apparent	clear, plain
appreciable	many
appropriate	(omit), proper, right
approximately	about
as a means of	to
ascertain	find out, learn
as prescribed by	in, under
assist, assistance	aid, help
attain	meet
attempt	try
at the present time	at present, now
be advised	(omit)
benefit	help
by means of	by, with
capability	ability, can
close proximity	near
combat environment	combat
combined	joint
commence	begin
comply with	follow
component	part
comprise	form, include, make up
concerning	about, on
consequently	so
consolidate	combine, join, merge
constitutes	is, forms, makes up
contains	has
convene	meet
currently	now
deem	believe, consider, think
delete	cut, drop
demonstrate	prove, show
depart	leave
designate	appoint, choose, name
desire	want, wish
determine	decide, figure, find
disclose	show
discontinue	drop, stop

Instead of	Try
disseminate	give, issue, pass, send
due to the fact that	due to, since
during the period	during
effect modifications	make changes
elect	choose, pick
eliminate	cut, drop, end
employ	use
encounter	meet
endeavor	try
ensure	make sure
enumerate	count
equipments	equipment
equitable	fair
equivalent	equal
establish	set up, prove, show
evidenced	showed
evident	clear
exhibit	show
expedite	hasten, speed up
expeditious	fast, quick
expend	spend
expertise	ability, skill
expiration	end
facilitate	ease, help
failed to	didn't
feasible	can be done
females	women
finalize	complete, finish
for a period of	for
for example,____etc.	for example, such as
forfeit	give up, lose
for the purpose of	for, to
forward	send
frequently	often
function	act, role, work
furnish	give, send
has a requirement for	needs
herein	here

Instead of	Try
heretofore	until now
herewith	below, here
however	but
identical	same
identify	find, name, show
immediately	at once
impacted	affected, changed
implement	carry out, start
in accordance with	by, following, per, under
in addition	also, besides, too
in an effort to	to
inasmuch as	since
in a timely manner	on time, promptly
inception	start
inform	tell
indicate	show, write down
indication	sign
initial	first
initiate	start
in lieu of	instead of
in order that	for, so
in order to	to
in regard to	about, concerning, on
inter alia	(omit)
interface with	meet, work with
interpose no objection	don't object
in the amount of	for
in the event that	if
in the near future	shortly, soon
in the process of	(omit)
in view of	since
in view of the above	so
is applicable to	applies to
is authorized to	may
is in consonance with	agrees with, follows
is responsible for	(omit), handles
it appears	seems
it is	(omit)
it is essential	must, need to
it is requested	please, we request, I request

Instead of	Try
limited number	few
limitations	limits
magnitude	size
maintain	keep, support
majority of	most
maximum	greatest, largest, most
methodology	method
minimize	decrease, lessen, reduce
minimum	least, smallest
modify	change
monitor	check, watch
necessitate	cause, need
notify	let know, tell
not later than 10 May	by 10 May, before 11 May
not later than 1600	by 1600
notwithstanding	in spite of, still
numerous	many
objective	aim, goal
obligate	bind, compel
observe	see
on a _____ basis	(omit)
operate	run, use, work
optimum	best, greatest, most
option	choice, way
parameters	limits
participate	take part
perform	do
permit	let
pertaining to	about, of, on
point in time	point, time
portion	part
possess	have, own
practicable	practical
preclude	prevent
previously	before
prioritize	rank
prior to	before
proceed	do, go ahead, try

Instead of	Try
procure	buy
proficiency	skill
provide	give, offer, say
provided that	if
provides guidance for	guides
purchase	buy
pursuant to	by, following, per, under
reflect	say, show
regarding	about, of on
relative to	about, on
relocate	move
remain	stay
remainder	rest
remuneration	pay, payment
render	give, make
represents	is
requests	ask
require	must, need
requirement	need
reside	live
retain	keep
said, some, such (e.g. "said amount")	the, this, that
selection	choice
set forth in	in
similar to	like
solicit	ask for, request
state-of-the-art	latest
subject	the, this, your
submit	give, send
subsequent	later, next
subsequently	after, later, then
substantial	large, much
successfully complete	complete, pass
sufficient	enough
take action to	(omit)
task	ask
terminate	end, stop
the month of	(omit)
there are	(omit), exist

Instead of	*Try*
therefore	so
therein	there
there is	(omit), exists
thereof	its, their
the undersigned	I
the use of	(omit)
timely	prompt
time period	(either one)
transmit	send
under the provisions of	under
until such time as	until
validate	confirm
viable	practical
vice	instead of, versus
warrant	call for, permit
whereas	because, since
with reference to	about
with the exception of	except for
witnessed	saw
your office	you

ACTION VERBS

act	attain	compute
activate	audit	conduct
adapt	budget	confront
address	build	conserve
adopt	calculate	consolidate
advertise	catalogue	construct
advise	change	consult
analyze	chart	contract
anticipate	classify	control
apply	coach	coordinate
appraise	collect	correspond
arrange	communicate	counsel
assembly	compile	create
assess	complete	defer

assist	compose	define
delegate	forward	negotiate
deliver	gather	observe
demonstrate	govern	obtain
design	guide	operate
detail	head	order
detect	help	organize
determine	hire	originate
develop	identify	paint
devise	illustrate	participate
diagnose	improve	perfect
direct	index	perform
discover	indoctrinate	persuade
dispense	influence	photograph
display	inform	pilot
disprove	initiate	pioneer
dissect	innovate	plan
distribute	inspect	play
divert	inspire	predict
draft	install	prepare
dramatize	institute	prescribe
edit	instruct	preserve
educate	integrate	preside
effect	interpret	print
electrify	interview	process
eliminate	introduce	produce
enforce	invent	program
enlarge	inventory	project
entertain	investigate	promote
estimate	judge	propose
evaluate	lead	protect
examine	lecture	provide
exhibit	maintain	publicize
expand	manage	purchase
explain	map	quote
express	market	raise
extract	measure	reason
familiarize	mediate	recommend
figure	model	reconcile
file	modify	record
filter	monitor	recruit
fix	motivate	reduce
formulate	navigate	refer

render
reorganize
repair
replace
report
represent
research
resolve
respond
restore
retrieve
review
revise
rewrite
save
schedule
select

simplify
sketch
solve
sort
spark
specify
stimulate
streamline
strengthen
study
suggest
summarize
supervise
supply
survey
synthesize

tabulate
talk
test
time
train
transcribe
transfer
translate
transmit
treat
tutor
unify
update
upgrade
vitalize
write

BRIEF BIBLIOGRAPHY
FOR BUSINESS WRITERS

Bates, Jefferson D. *Writing with Precision.* 6th ed. Washington, D. C.: Acropolis Books, Ltd. 1993. Gives clear explanations. It takes off where Strunk and White leave off.

Buzan, Tony. *Use Both Sides of Your Brain.* New York: E. P. Dutton, Inc., 1983. New techniques on reading, studying, and thinking. Includes an excellent discussion of mindmapping.

Hodges, John C., Winifred Bryan Horner, Suzanne Strobeck Webb, and Robert Keith Miller. *Harbrace College Handbook.* 12th ed. Fort Worth: Harcourt Brace College Publishers, 1994. One of the most comprehensive and correct guides for the individual writer and college instructor.

Jordan, Lewis. *The New York Times Manual of Style and Usage.* New York: Times Books, 1976. An enlarged edition of guidelines for those who write and edit. Easy to use and very complete.

Noble, David F. *Gallery of Best Resumes.* Indianapolis:JIST Works, Inc., 1994. New ideas and formats on resume writing.

Sabin, William A. *The Gregg Reference Manual,* 6th ed. New York: Gregg Division/McGraw-Hill Book Company, 1985.

Strunk, William, Jr., and E.B. White. *The Elements of Style.* 3rd ed. New York: Macmillan Company, 1979. Probably the best and briefest statement of the principal requirements for plain English.

Warriner, John E., Mary E. Whitten, and Francis Griffith. *English Grammar and Composition.* New York: Harcourt Brace Jovanovich, 1977. Extensive grammatical explanations, rules of composition, and practice exercises to improve writing.

Webster's New World Misspeller's Dictionary. New York: Simon and Schuster, 1983. 15,000 common misspellings and their correct spellings. Unique and valuable reference guide.

INDEX

More Good Books by JIST Works, Inc.

How To Write Complaint Letters That Work

A Consumer's Guide to Resolving Conflicts & Getting Results—
Writing Effective Complaint Letters
By Patricia H. Westheimer and Jim Mastro

Effective complaint letters are one of the best methods of resolving conflicts and getting results. This informative book explains how to write results-oriented complaint letters, including advice on:

6 x 9, Paper, 210 pp.
ISBN 1-57112-063-7
$12.95—Order Code HWCL

- Finding the right person to address
- Deciding when a complaint letter is appropriate
- Determining the proper tone

Sales Information

- Sample letters included
- Outlines how to resolve typical consumer and business conflicts
- Assists you in finding the right person . . . when a letter is ignored

Face-to-Face Selling

By Bart Breighner

The author, founder and president of a successful art sales company, shares his unique sales success formula and talks straight about face-to-face selling. Entry-level salespeople will learn:

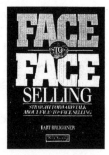

- The art of convincing
- How to show a prospect the value of the product
- How to close the sale

6 x 9, Paper, 240 pp.
ISBN 1-57112-065-3
$9.95—Order Code FFS

Other Information:

- Tips on selling one-on-one and to groups
- Real-life examples of successful techniques
- Includes sound principles for effective phone work and a sample presentation

*Look for these and other fine books from **JIST Works, Inc.***
at your full service bookstore, or call us for additional information.

More Good Books by JIST Works, Inc.
Mind Your Own Business!

Sould you go into business for yourself?
Can you be an entrepreneur?
By LaVerne Ludden, Ed.D. / Bonnie Maitlen, Ed.,D.

Two successful entrepreneurs answer these and other crucial questions those who dream of starting their own business should ask themselves. Covers the basics of starting a new business or becoming self-employed. Practical questionnaires, assessment forms, worksheets, and checklists make this an invaluable handbook for the "wanna-be" entrepreneur.

6 x 9, Paper, 224 pp. • ISBN 1-56370-083-2 • **$9.95** • Order Code MYOB

Sales Information

- Both authros are successful entrepreneurs
- Both are qualified, experienced trainers, and adult educators
- Currently being used by a national professional outplacement firm

The Customer is Usually Wrong!

Contrary to What You've Been Told . . .
What You Know to Be true about Customer Service!
By Fred E. Jandt

Emphasizing the use of win-win negotiation skills, this revolutionary book explains why the popular adage, "The customer is always right," has failed. Includes a frank discussion of customer expectations and what type of service works are actually able to provide. Also includes:
  - Real-life examples of effective supervision
    and positive employee morale
  - A Model Service Organization

8-1/2 x 11, Paper, 160 pp.
ISBN 1-57112-067-X
$12.95 Order Code CUR

Other Information:

- Important training tool for every customer service representative and supervisor
- Demonstrates effective supervision and positive employee morale
- Provides actual examples of the win-win strategies at work in a customer service setting.

*Look for these and other fine books from **JIST Works, Inc.***
at your full service bookstore, or call us for additional information.

JIST publishes a variety of books on careers and job search topics. Please consider ordering one or more books from your dealer, local bookstore, or directly from JIST.

Orders from Individuals: Simply send your order to our fax number **1-317-264-3709** or **1-800-JIST-FAX** or call **1-317-264-3720.** Our offices are open weekdays 7 a.m. to 7 p.m. eastern standard time.

QTY	BOOK TITLE	TOTAL
	America's 50 Fastest Growing Jobs: *The Authoritative Information Source* • ISBN: 1-56370-091-3 • **$11.95**	
	America's Top 300 Jobs: A Complete Career Handbook *(trade version of the Occupational Outlook Handbook)* • ISBN 1-56370-163-4 • **$17.95**	
	America's Top Jobs for College Graduates: *Detailed Information on Jobs and Trends for College Grads — and Those Considering A College Education* • ISBN 1-56370-140-5 • **$14.95**	
	The Career Connection for College Education: *A Guide to College Majors & Related Career Opportunities* • ISBN 1-56370-142-1 • **$16.95**	
	The Career Connection for Technical Education: *A Guide to Technical Training & Related Career Opportunities* • ISBN 1-56370-143-X • **$14.95**	
	The Complete Guide for Occupational Exploration: Up-to-Date Information on More Than 12,000 Occupations *(soft cover)* • ISBN 1-56370-052-2 • **$34.95;** *(hard cover)* • ISBN 1-56370-100-6 • **$44.95**	
	Gallery of Best Resumes: *A Collection of Quality Resumes by Professional Resume Writers* • ISBN 1-56370-144-8 • **$16.95**	
	Getting the Job You Really Want: *A Step-by-Step Guide* • ISBN 1-56370-092-1 • **$9.95**	
	Job Strategies for Professionals: *A Survival Guide for Experienced White-Collar Workers* • ISBN 1-56370-139-1 • **$9.95**	
	Mind Your Own Business: *Getting Started as an Entrepreneur* • ISBN 1-56370-083-2 • **$9.95**	
	Occupational Outlook Handbook 1994-1995 Edition • ISBN 1-56370-160-X • **$15.95** *(soft cover)* ISBN 1-56370-161-8 • **$21.95** *(hard cover)*	
	The Quick Interview and Salary Negotiation Book: *Dramatically Improve Your Interviewing Skill — and Pay — in a Matter of Hours* • ISBN 1-56370-162-6 • **$9.95**	
	The Quick Resume and Cover Letter Book: *Write and Use an Effective Resume in Only One Day* • ISBN 1-56370-141-3 • **$9.95**	
	The Very Quick Job Search: *Get a Good Job in Less Time* • ISBN 1-56370-181-2 • **$12.95**	
	The Resume Solution: *How to Write and Use a Resume That Gets Results* • ISBN 1-56370-180-4 • **$9.95**	
	Dictionary of Occupational Titles: *2-Volume Set* • ISBN 1-56370-000-X • **$39.00**	